PERSONNEL UTILIZATION IN LIBRARIES:
A SYSTEMS APPROACH

Prepared for

The Illinois Library Task Analysis Project

by

MYRL RICKING

and

ROBERT E. BOOTH

Published in cooperation with the
ILLINOIS STATE LIBRARY by the AMERICAN LIBRARY ASSOCIATION
Chicago 1974

An (LSCA Title I) Research Project
  Funded by the
ILLINOIS STATE LIBRARY
  and supervised jointly by the
ILLINOIS LIBRARY ASSOCIATION
THE LIBRARY EDUCATION DIVISION
  and the
LIBRARY ADMINISTRATION DIVISION
  of the
AMERICAN LIBRARY ASSOCIATION

Library of Congress Cataloging in
Publication Data

Ricking, Myrl.
    Personnel utilization in libraries.

    Bibliography: p.
    1. Library personnel management.
I. Booth, Robert Edmond, 1917-
joint author. II. Illinois Library Task
Analysis Project. III. Illinois. State
Library, Springfield. IV. Title.
Z682.R5   658.3'7'02   74-8688
ISBN 0-8389-3155-3

CONTENTS

ILLUSTRATIONS

FOREWORD

In the late 1960s nearly all professions in the United States thought they faced severe shortages of manpower in their fields, both in professional and supporting areas. Librarianship was not immune: there was more work to be done than existing staffs could do; there were budgeted professional vacancies that could not be filled. And, concurrently, there were concerns being quietly expressed that some of the shortages could be ameliorated by a changed utilization of existing manpower.

It was at this time and out of these concerns that Julius R. Chitwood, then president of the Illinois Library Association, appointed an ad hoc Committee on Manpower Training and Utilization to study patterns of staff assignments and to recommend to library administrators more effective ways of utilizing professional staff. After examining the use of professional staff in a few libraries, however, it became clear to this committee of volunteer researchers that they could not do the job which needed doing. It was also clear that a need was there, that a small segment of the library manpower problem could be more fully explored, that the results of a serious study in Illinois might have national implications, and that the resources for such a study should be sought.

The Illinois group joined with representatives of the Library Administration Division and the Library Education Division of the American Library Association (ALA) to design a study which would examine the work actually being performed in libraries, would relate this to the kinds of training such work required, and would disseminate this information to the library community at large. The first proposal for an Illinois Library Task Analysis Project (ILTAP) was submitted to the Illinois State Library in 1969 for possible funding under the Library Services and Construction Act.

Such funding was obtained and the Social, Educational Research and Development, Inc. (SERD) of Silver Spring, Maryland, was engaged to conduct a task analysis of work being performed by individuals—regardless of their job titles—in representative libraries in Illinois. This was the first study (Phase I) of what was to become a three-phase project. From the very beginning, ILTAP has been sustained by the vital interest of the Illinois State Library and its director, Alphonse F. Trezza. The financial support from the library has made the project possible; the intellectual support of Al Trezza has helped shape its direction and sustained all concerned with it in periods of doubt.

Phase I of the project, performed by SERD, identified 1,615 tasks performed by 116 individuals in eighteen libraries of various types and sizes in Illinois.[1] Each task was rated according to fifteen scales, producing some

1. Social, Educational Research and Development, Inc., *A Task Analysis of Library Jobs in the State of Illinois* (ERIC no. ED 040 723, 1970). The participating libraries were:

400,000 bits of data. In all probability this is the first study that has attempted to apply the methods and techniques of functional job analysis to libraries. It provides a realistic description of work actually being done in public, school, academic, and special libraries, even if a few of the evaluations the contractor assigned to tasks caused some in the profession to question the methodology.

Useful as the SERD-generated data could be, they were difficult to use in the form of the Phase I report to the Advisory Committee. The second phase of ILTAP, therefore, had as its goal the interpretation of the data in ways that would be more widely useful to the profession. Did the tasks identified by SERD interface with the categories of personnel in the ALA policy statement *Library Education and Manpower*?[2] Did the training levels the contractor assigned to tasks suggest new staff utilization patterns? Did librarians working in libraries agree that SERD's evaluations were correct? What did the SERD study have to say about organizing staff responsibilities in different types of libraries?

Three consultants, each with extensive experience in libraries, were identified and engaged to examine and test the SERD data from the points of view of public, school, and academic libraries respectively, with the primary objective of testing the validity of the *Library Education and Manpower* statement.

Dale Canelas' study focused on 990 academic library tasks, deleting only those tasks which could not take place in an academic library.

> The tasks [were] grouped by (1) function (i.e., administration, catalog, reference, etc.) and within it by (2) training time order (the amount of formal education plus on-the-job training that is required for the performance of a given task), and arranged in 'task clusters' by performance level—that is, clerical, professional, etc. The data was then analyzed to produce . . . profiles of the varied intellectual, educational and judgmental qualifications required by categories of library jobs. The job summaries define position levels, list the duties and qualifications determined by SERD, and comment upon these findings from the point of view of a practicing academic librarian.

(school libraries) Alton Community Unit School, District 11, Alton; Barrington Middle School, District 4, Barrington; Highland Elementary School, District 68, Skokie; Highland Park High School, District 113, Highland Park; Old Orchard Junior High School, District 68, Skokie; (public libraries) Aurora Public Library, Aurora; East St. Louis Public Library, East St. Louis; Highland Park Public Library, Highland Park; Rockford Public Library, Rockford; (special libraries) Argonne National Laboratories, Argonne; J. Walter Thompson Advertising Agency, Chicago; Veterans Administration Hospital, Hines; (college and university libraries) College of DuPage, Glen Ellyn; Quincy College, Quincy; Southern Illinois University, Carbondale; (other) Illinois Materials Resource Processing Center, Rockford; Illinois State Library, Springfield; Northern Illinois Library System, Rockford.

2. *Library Education and Manpower,* A Statement of Policy Adopted by the Council of the American Library Association, June 30, 1970 (Chicago: ALA Office for Library Education, 1970); included here as Appendix D.

The advantage of this approach is that the task clusters can be used by administrators as a basis for evaluating and realigning present positions or constructing future positions in a wide variety of work situations. It allows the supervisor to choose those tasks appropriate to his own departmental function whereas a job description written for a hypothetical position may or may not be applicable to his situation. A second advantage is that clustering all like tasks in each functional area regardless of the number of positions that may be needed to perform such duties in a given library circumstance makes it possible to analyze the data on the basis of all the work performed in that area and draw conclusions applicable to a wide range of positions engaged in similar functions.[3]

The report by Bernice Wiese focused on supporting jobs in school library media systems; and used the following design for analyzing the SERD data.

1. A total of 727 tasks relating to functions in a school library was identified, representing both supporting and professional tasks and thus allowing for the development of a career lattice for a school library media system.
2. Training time was chosen as the basic dimension for evaluating tasks. Other factors selected to compare and relate to training time were general educational development (reasoning, mathematics, language), worker functions (data, people, things), worker instructions, and task environment.
3. Each task was evaluated in terms of these five factors and in terms of the correlation and interrelation of the scalings. Disagreements with the SERD codings were noted, but no changes made in the scalings at this stage in the analysis.
4. Two-dimensional matrixes were developed to identify areas of correlation of training time with each of the other four factors and to point up significant areas of skills and knowledge. . . . All of the original SERD scalings were maintained to show how management analysts viewed the levels of complexity of tasks in library situations.
5. Tasks related to audio-visual materials, equipment, services, and programs were sorted to determine the kind of task for a specialized job in media technology for the supporting staff. . . . The functional area codings in SERD for cataloging and processing tasks provided sufficient information for considering specialized tasks in this area.
6. Tasks relating to knowledge and training in technical library skills and graduate library training were sorted to aid in decisions on recoding training time for some tasks and also for guidance in developing suggestions for training programs.

3. Dale Brunelle Canelas, *Task Analysis of Library Jobs in the State of Illinois: A Working Paper on the Relevance of the Study to Academic Libraries* (ERIC no. ED 067 113, 1971), p. 2.

7. An analysis was made of the statistical tables and the implications for career lattices, job descriptions, training programs, and instructional materials.[4]

The study by Myrl Ricking related to tasks performed in public libraries.

A model was to be developed in which the tasks would be arranged in accordance with the definitions established in the policy statement, on the basis of the consultant's experience and judgment, and bearing in mind the scaling of all appropriate factors by SERD. This would be the exact process which would have to be followed by an administrator attempting to apply the new manpower policy in an individual library, and the result, besides serving as a test of the policy's validity, should also serve as a demonstration to administrators of how to make such application to positions in their own libraries.[5]

The reports of the three consultants were reviewed by a panel of educators, personnel specialists, library administrators, social scientists, and librarians from the four major types of libraries and from many parts of the country. The review panel found all four of the ILTAP documents to be of considerable significance, but, again, not in a format that would encourage wide use. The panel in its report recommended that an improved substitute for the out-of-print 1948 ALA *Descriptive List of Professional and Nonprofessional Duties in Libraries* be prepared which would provide a synthesis of the data in the SERD and Phase II consultants' reports, could be field-tested in a number of libraries, and would be generally available as a tool for the profession.[6]

Myrl Ricking and Robert E. Booth, both with prior experience in ILTAP, were engaged to produce such a document. Miss Ricking had produced, as a consultant, a working paper for Phase II; Dr. Booth had served as a Library Education Division (LED) representative to the Advisory Committee in Phases I and II of ILTAP. The first draft was prepared for use in workshops at the fall, 1972, meetings of the Illinois, New York, and California state library associations. Many questions arose from these meetings, followed by detailed and extensive reevaluations of all parts of the draft.

We learned as we proceeded that we should have started at a different point from the one we used; that the definition of goals must come before the identification of tasks; that tasks derive from programs, programs develop in response to stated goals, stated goals come from the assessment of needs. We developed a systems approach.

We came to realize that an understanding of the process is more important

---

4. M. Bernice Wiese, *Proposals for an Organizational Model, Job Descriptions, and Training Programs for the Supporting Staff of School Library Media Systems* (ERIC no. ED 067 112, 1971), p. 9.

5. Myrl Ricking, *Illinois Library Task Analysis Project: Phase II, A Study* (ERIC no. ED 067 111, 1971), p. 1; included here as Appendix E.

6. Illinois Library Task Analysis Project, "Project Proposal and Summary of the Discussion and Recommendations of the Review Panel for Phase II" (Meeting in Chicago, Oct. 21-23, 1971, ERIC no. ED 067 110).

than a task list which may result from it; that the methodology, rather than the product, is likely to be of most help in the field. This Phase III document is thus a synthesis, rather than a summary, of all the preceding phases, including the reactions and criticisms of the deeply interested workshop participants.

Its greatest use will probably be in small to medium-sized public and college libraries and in school libraries. This is not merely because the research upon which it is based was carried out in small to medium-sized libraries, but perhaps more because libraries of this size often do not have the personnel resources to perform the type of analysis this study provides. This does not deny its usefulness to libraries of any size, nor does it deny its usefulness to any librarian seeking an opportunity to analyze more carefully his or her own work.

We hope that the publication will help administrators in all kinds of libraries to define more effective ways to use professional/technical/clerical staffs and that it will help staffs identify the kinds of activities which are typical of their training backgrounds. Library school faculty and students should also find the study of value. Most importantly, we hope that it will help all concerned with libraries to define more clearly what it is that we are about.

Finally, in a document concerned with utilization of human talent, it is appropriate to mention a few of the very talented human beings who have helped us along the way, although by no means can we mention all. Mary Cashman, her Personnel Committee in the New York Library Association, and John Humphry provided early and valuable critical assessments of our work in the New York Library Association meeting. Richard Johnson and Stefan Moses helped us in the California Library Association workshop sessions; Ethel Crockett, the California State Librarian, maintains an interest in what we are doing. And, over the years, the presidents of the Illinois Library Association have been part of our Advisory Committee and helped us maintain regular contact with the field. These were: Julius Chitwood, Mary Ann Swanson, de Lafayette Reid, Joe W. Kraus, Donald E. Wright, and Peter Bury. To these, and many, many others, we offer our thanks.

ILLINOIS LIBRARY TASK ANALYSIS PROJECT

Advisory Committee:

LESTER ASHEIM
JULIUS R. CHITWOOD
RUTH FRAME
MARY QUINT
AGNES REAGAN
BARRY SIMON
BARBARA SLANKER
DELORES VAUGHAN
THOMAS M. BROWN, Chairman

Chapter 1

TASK IDENTIFICATION
AND ANALYSIS

Any analytical approach to the recruitment, educational preparation, and utilization of personnel—in libraries or any other occupational field—must begin with an analysis of the work to be performed.

Analysis of the nature of the work precedes the determination of both the kinds of personnel needed and the kinds of educational preparation they should have.

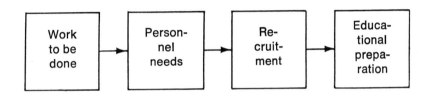

For decades library managers have been engaged in one form or another of position or job analysis—a process of determining for individual positions and groups of positions the skills, levels of responsibility, and knowledge required.[1] The process has been thought of primarily as position classification, since its chief purpose was the evaluation of positions, as measured by objective standards against others in the organization. And the principal objective of such evaluation was an equitable scale of compensation, or "equal pay for equal work."

What ILTAP has been concerned with, however, is analysis on a task-by-task basis of the work performed—not primarily for purposes of such comparative evaluation, but to reveal more clearly the nature of the work itself in terms of its demands for skills, aptitudes, and knowledge on the part of the worker.[2] Obviously, there is a direct relationship between the two approaches, and a brief glimpse at the history of job evaluation in the United States may help to clarify their relationship.

Although this history goes back at least to World War I, the strong surge of interest did not come until World War II. However, from the beginning, industry and government (including most libraries) have followed different paths. Business and industry, on the whole, moved in the direction of factor-comparison and point-evaluation plans, generally described as "quantitative" (or numerical, scientific, or objective). Government and the academic community generally followed position-classification or "non-quantitative" methods.

1. *See* Glossary for distinction between *position* and *job*.
2. *See* Glossary for *task*.

All quantitative methods involve a formal breakdown of a job or position into the specific factors that contribute to its value, or weight, and the assignment of certain finite values, usually numerical, to these factors. The non-quantitative methods include the ranking method, the grade-standard method, and the position-classification method, all of which involve comparing entire jobs or positions with grade standards, comparable jobs in the labor market, or with each other. The ALA publication, *Position Classification and Salary Administration in Libraries,* gives a good exposition of the methodology of position classification still in use in most libraries today.[3] The grade-standard method is epitomized by the U.S. Civil Service Commission *Position Classification Standards,* used for many years by federal libraries.[4]

In Phase I of ILTAP, SERD used a quantitative method; the scales, or factors, which they used can be seen in Appendix A. The Manpower Administration of the U.S. Department of Labor has developed a structure of worker functions, indicating a relationship to data, people, and things arranged in hierarchies according to a numeric scale.[5]

At the present writing, the U.S. Civil Service Commission is also studying a quantitative factor-ranking method involving the identification of "benchmark" jobs which will serve as guides in the use and assignment of evaluation scores.[6]

WHY FACTOR ANALYSIS?

The position-evaluation methodology long used by libraries has generally served its purpose fairly well, and it can be used just as objectively as a factor-analysis system. Even for purposes of position classification, however, the quantitative methods have certain advantages:

1. By requiring scrutiny of all factors, they lessen the possibility of over-looking some elements or of basing evaluation on one or more predominant characteristics without balancing all
2. By the uniform application of predetermined values, they insure the measuring of all tasks or positions against the same yardstick or on the same scales
3. They tend to eliminate, or at least lessen, intuitive judgments and conscious or unconscious bias on the part of raters

3. ALA Board on Personnel Administration, *Position Classification and Salary Administration in Libraries* (Chicago: The Association, 1951).

4. *See* "Guide for the Classification of Positions Providing Professional-Level Library and Information Services," Transmittal Sheet 60, February 1966; and "Library Technician Series," Transmittal Sheet 62, June 1966 (Washington, D.C.; Govt. Print. Off.).

5. U.S. Dept. of Labor, Manpower Administration, *Handbook for Analyzing Jobs* (Washington, D.C.: Govt. Print. Off., 1972). *See* Appendix B.

6. U.S. Civil Service Commission, *Report of the Job Evaluation and Pay Review Task Force,* vol. 2: *Models of Evaluation Systems and Pay Structures* (published as committee report with distribution to selected federal agencies, 1970, and reprinted by the House of Representatives Committee on Post Office and Civil Service, Subcommittee on Employee Benefits, Committee Print no. 16, 92nd Cong., 2nd sess., Jan. 12, 1972). *See* Appendix C.

4. They require that the elements, or degrees, of only one factor be held in mind at any one time, thus aiding the rater and preventing a "blurring" of several factors in his evaluation
5. Any differences among raters are localized to one or more elements of established factors, thus facilitating discussion and resolution of differences
6. The evaluation of separate components and the expression of such evaluation in numerical scores also assists in the explanation of the rater's judgments to the incumbents and supervisors of the positions being rated.

Although factor analysis has historically been criticized as being more things-related than the more generalized methodologies and thus less well suited to the analysis of professional work, contemporary usage demonstrates clearly that its applicability is not so limited.

JOB RESTRUCTURING

Even more important than the considerations outlined above, however, is the fact that task analysis of the sort undertaken by ILTAP provides an approach to the improved utilization of staff which the more generalized methods do not. When the analysis is made at the task level, with each task rated separately with respect to a variety of factors, it becomes possible to regroup or rearrange the tasks in accordance with new combinations of the factors involved.

Thus any task in the list identified, described, and analyzed by SERD could be grouped with others in these terms:

1. Who or what sets the standards
2. The degree of quality required
3. The pace of the work
4. The environment in which the task occurs
5. Its relationship to data, people, or things
6. The reasoning, mathematics, and language skills required
7. The nature and degree of instructions provided the worker
8. The training time required in order to perform the task
9. The time required to complete the task
10. The physical demands
11. The knowledge, skills, and abilities required

In other words, task analysis provides the basis for *job restructuring,* or *job design* as it is often called. Job restructuring is the technique of breaking down jobs into their smallest components and putting these components back together again in new combinations to achieve certain objectives.

Among these objectives may be:

1. That each job contribute as effectively as possible to the achievement of the goals of the organization
2. That the jobs can be filled by people locally available with the required knowledge and skills

3. That the highest knowledge and skill elements be concentrated in the fewest possible jobs, especially in occupations where manpower is limited

4. That the resulting jobs also serve the goals of the individuals filling them in terms of interest and self-development.[7]

IDENTIFICATION AND DESCRIPTION OF TASKS

Obviously, before tasks can be analyzed and structured into jobs, they must first be *identified* and then *described.* In a new organization or unit thereof, the tasks can logically be derived from the goals to be achieved, in a descending hierarchy of objectives, programs, functions, and tasks. In an on-going operation, however, the first step is usually the identification of tasks actually being performed, and this was the approach taken by SERD in Phase I of ILTAP.

This identification may be done in a variety of ways, including the keeping by the worker of minute-by-minute records of tasks performed and time spent in their performance; the completion of questionnaires by incumbents, listing the major tasks performed; side-by-side observation by analysts of work in progress; or, as in the case of SERD, on-the-scene interviews conducted by job analysts. Combinations of these methods are frequently used.

The description of the work which is done may be broken down in various ways and to various degrees, moving through broad functions to specific tasks, defined by SERD as "the smallest item of work, action, or activity involved in a job," and by the Department of Labor as ". . . one or more elements (the smallest step into which it is practicable to subdivide any work activity without analyzing separate motions, movements, and mental processes involved) and one of the distinct activities that constitute logical and necessary steps in the performance of work by the worker."[8]

Most libraries follow the pattern of identifying rather broadly stated duties, not unlike those in the ALA *Descriptive List,* in the form of job descriptions.[9] These are specific, but not detailed. They indicate the primary tasks performed, but do not identify the separate elements of which they are made up.

Similarly, there are different approaches that may be taken to the description of the work performed, ranging from the individual's own choice of words to describe his work, through the rather generalized but widely accepted terminology appearing in most library job descriptions, to the highly explicit terminology of the U.S. Department of Labor. The approach used by SERD was midway on this scale of refinement, utilizing, for the most part, methods verbs, but not a controlled structure and vocabulary.

---

7. A thorough treatment of job restructuring is found in *A Handbook for Job Restructuring,* U.S. Dept. of Labor, Manpower Administration (Washington, D.C.: Govt. Print. Off., 1970).

8. Dept. of Labor, *Handbook for Analyzing Jobs,* p. 3.

9. ALA Board on Personnel Administration, *Descriptive List of Professional and Nonprofessional Duties in Libraries* (Chicago: The Association, 1948).

ANALYSIS OF TASKS

The process of *analysis* involves the application of the appropriate set of scales to the tasks that have been identified and described. Whether the analysis is in terms of the Department of Labor's data, people, and things; the factors proposed by the Civil Service Commission's Job Evaluation and Pay Review Task Force; or the SERD scales, the process is essentially the same: the evaluation by an individual or a team of analysts of each task or function against the scales being used. The application of the SERD scales to the tasks identified in Phase I as being performed in the public library is included here as Appendix E, in order to illustrate the process.

Task analysis is not a simple process, and it can only be as useful as the persons performing it are skilled. Jobs and tasks are not tangible entities susceptible of absolute measurement, and all systems of analysis, even the most highly quantified, are ultimately dependent on the judgment of the rater. In fact, using the most objective of systems, it is possible for two or more equally competent analysts, applying the same criteria and measurements to the same tasks, to arrive at different evaluations. The ultimate test of any system is the extent to which it minimizes this possibility.

The three basic requirements of a job analyst are:

1. Objectivity
2. Thorough understanding of, and experience in, the methodology employed
3. Thorough knowledge of the work being described.

The last may well require study beyond the mere obtaining of information from the persons performing the work. One of the dangers of librarians performing their own task analysis lies in the natural tendency to understand and appreciate their own, i.e. professional, work to a greater degree than they do that of other categories of personnel.

One of the determinants of which system is used, if the analysis is to be done internally, is the ability of the staff to use it. The Department of Labor methodology, for example, requires a considerably more sophisticated level of training than does the one used by SERD. Which system is selected depends on the nature of the organization, its needs and problems, and the resources of both time and money it is able and willing to expend on the process. The primary determinant is, of course, the use to which the analysis is to be put. There is no value whatever in the most highly developed analysis if its objectives and uses have not been determined before it is undertaken.

Furthermore, along with competent evaluation personnel, any task analysis program requires for its success:

1. A supervisory force that understands and believes in its usefulness
2. Employees who recognize the need for and benefits of such a program
3. A top management with awareness that task analysis is neither a cure-all nor a one-shot operation, but an effective management mechanism that requires continuing attention and support.

Chapter 2

ASSESSING THE LIBRARY'S OBJECTIVES

The Illinois Library Task Analysis Project began with—indeed consisted of—the kind of task analysis described in the preceding chapter. And this is where most libraries begin, and often end, their analysis of the work performed within the agency. It became very clear, however, in both Phase II and Phase III of the project that tasks could not be structured into jobs and career patterns without the framework of an organization of which they were a part.

One of the studies most influential in the thinking of the committee in this regard was *A Systems Approach to New Careers* by W. W. Wiley and Sidney A. Fine.[1] In it, six steps are described and defined as shown in figure 1.

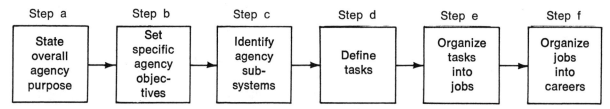

Fig. 1. The systems approach of Wiley and Fine

In other words, just as one cannot make appropriate selection of staff until the skills and knowledges required are well understood, so the skill and knowledge requirements cannot be arrived at without, as the first step, a clear understanding of the goals to which they are to be directed.

Systems analysis has been defined as ". . . a formal procedure for examining a complex process or organization, reducing it to its component parts, and relating these parts to each other and to the unit as a whole in accordance with an agreed-upon performance criterion."[2] The process involves a continuous review and modification of activities in a logical and strongly patterned approach.

To begin with tasks is to begin in the middle rather than at the beginning, and the organization taking a fresh look at its utilization of personnel must first proceed through a number of other highly complex steps in a methodical sequence.

1. W. W. Wiley and Sidney A. Fine, *A Systems Approach to New Careers* (Kalamazoo, Mich.: The W. E. Upjohn Institute for Employment Research, 1969).
2. Harold Borko, "Design of Information Systems and Services," in *Annual Review of Information Science and Technology* (Palo Alto: Annual Reviews, 1967), p. 37.

OVERALL AGENCY PURPOSE

There must be clear understanding and general acceptance of the central purpose of any agency by all concerned with it at every stage of the agency's life. By *central purpose* is meant the broadest conceptualization of the reason or reasons for the creation and continuing existence of an agency, i.e., its mission. Many agencies will be able to identify a single central purpose. Some may have two or three central purposes in a closely knit cluster.

The conceptualization must be stated as specifically as possible in terms that will permit reasonable assessment of accomplishments. For example, the central purpose of the public library might be expressed as "to promote enlightened citizenship and to enrich personal life."[3] A more measurable purpose would be "to serve the community as a reliable source of information."

GOALS AND OBJECTIVES

Once a statement of central purpose has been established, the identification of *goals* can be examined. Any agency can have multiple goals from which *objectives* can be derived.

The literature relating to central purposes, goals, and objectives is extensive. It is also confusing, primarily because of a lack of consistency in the use of terminology. The position is taken here that there is a hierarchy of purposes, goals, and objectives as shown in figure 2. One of the most useful sources advocating the "hierarchy of objectives" theory is Granger.[4]

Central purpose may be defined as "the basic reason for an organization's existence," or as "the basis for functional unity, viewed by the organization as a whole, voiced by legitimate authority."[5] Goal can be defined as "a general target or aim from which several objectives are derived."[6] Objective is "an end result; a specific goal or target toward which effort is directed."[7]

Support for the formulation of library objectives is beginning to abound in the literature, notably, the five-year state plans for library service submitted by each state in the fall of 1972 to the U.S. Office of Education, Bureau of Libraries and Educational Technology, and the ALA Goals Study of 1972.[8] "Meeting the Challenge: Long Range Program for Library Development in

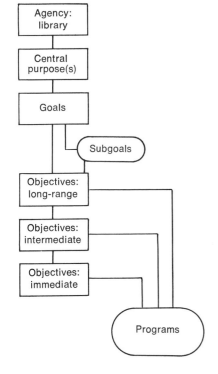

Fig. 2. A hierarchy of central purposes, goals, and objectives

3. Carlton B. Joeckel and Amy Winslow, *A National Plan for Public Library Service* (Chicago: American Library Assn., 1948), p. 16.

4. Charles H. Granger, "The Hierarchy of Objectives," *Harvard Business Review,* May-June 1964, p. 63-74.

5. John E. Roueche, George A. Baker III, and Richard L. Brownell, *Accountability and the Community College* (Washington, D.C.: American Assn. of Junior Colleges, 1971), p. 24; James G. March, *Handbook of Organizations* (Chicago: Rand-McNally, 1965), p. 1179.

6. Roueche, et al., *Accountability,* p. 24.

7. Ibid.

8. ALA Public Library Association, *A Strategy for Public Library Change* (Chicago: The Association, 1972).

Illinois, 1973-1978" provides a good illustration of the hierarchy of objectives advocated here, although also illustrating a differing approach to the terminology:

> The goal [central purpose] of the Illinois State Library is: The assured provision of excellent library service for all the residents of the state so that the need for cultural, educational, informational, and recreational resources can be met, and the governmental and economic development of the state can be fostered.

Three subgoals [goals] are then identified as:

1. The promotion and development of cooperative library networks operating regionally or statewide to provide effective coordination of library resources of public, academic, school, and special libraries
2. The promotion, support, and implementation of library services on a statewide basis for the cultural, educational, and economic development of the state and the inhabitants of the state
3. The promotion, support, implementation, and maintenance of library services on a state level for all state officers, offices, the General Assembly, the Judiciary, and all state agencies, bodies, and commissions.

Specific objectives may then be developed for each of the goals. An example, under Goal 1, would be:

Objective: Research new or better methods or routines of networking. Means to accomplish objective:

1. Study and explore delivery of interlibrary loan materials by December, 1973
2. Plan delivery system based on most efficient and fastest method by March, 1974
3. Implement plan by May, 1974
4. Study ways to improve means of location of materials by May, 1975
5. Study level of user needs in school, academic, special, and public libraries by October, 1976
6. Plan refinement of network based on studies by June, 1977
7. Implement refinements by January, 1978.[9]

NEEDS ASSESSMENT

Central purposes, goals, and objectives, if they are to have any meaning, must arise in direct response to need. In 1954, Abraham Maslow formulated a theory of motivation based upon the following hierarchy of needs:

> I. Physiological needs
> Food, water, sleep, shelter, sex

---

9. Illinois State Library, "Meeting the Challenge," *Illinois Libraries,* Nov.1972, p. 737-74. *See also* revisions in *Illinois Libraries,* Nov. 1973, p. 599-614.

II. Safety needs
Security, stability, protection; freedom from fear, anxiety, and chaos
III. Social needs
(a) Belongingness
(b) Love for others
IV. Esteem needs
(a) Strength, achievement, adequacy, mastery, competence, confidence in face of the world, freedom, independence
(b) Reputation, prestige, status, fame, glory, dominance, recognition, attention, importance, dignity, appreciation
V. Self-Actualization
"What a man can be, he must be.
To become everything that one is capable of becoming."[10]

These needs are related to each other in what Maslow calls "a hierarchy of prepotency." A person who is lacking food, safety, love, and esteem, will hunger for food more strongly than for anything else. But once a need is fairly well satisfied, the next higher need emerges. "The organism is dominated and its behavior organized only by unsatisfied needs."[11]

The Maslowian hierarchy poses important questions for the library in terms of where in the hierarchy we can accommodate the need for information, education, desires to know, to understand, and to explain. What do we we know about informational needs in different societies, e.g., technologically advanced vs. emerging? What do we know about information needs of different socio-economic groups or rural vs. urban communities? In librarianship, we are just beginning to ask these questions; we have few, if any, answers. To understand the process and role of librarianship, we must begin to devote greater effort to examining and reexamining societal needs as the fountainhead for the services and materials of the library. Needs must be studied first, and only then—in response to needs—can and should library services and resources be provided.

If an assessment of needs clearly indicates that all or part of the central purposes, goals, objectives, programs, and resources of a given library currently accepted or in use are not needed, then those purposes, goals, objectives, programs, and resources should change. Too many agencies are out of date, out of phase, and out of touch with the real needs of their client constituencies. As needs change, central purposes must change, as must all steps in the systems sequence.

In all too many library situations, we tend to start with existing services and resources and ask how we can restructure societal needs to fit what we currently provide as products, services, or other output. If society does not use

10. *Motivation and Personality* (New York: Harper, 1954); summarized from rev. ed. (New York: Harper & Row, 1970), p. 35-38.
11. Ibid., p. 38.

what we provide, or support what we propose, the fault is assumed to be with society and not with us. This is probably a common error of maturing or mature agencies which have failed to make recurring assessments of the needs for which they were created.

Harriett L. Robbins, Director of Evaluation of the former Evaluation Center of Ohio State University, suggests a framework for describing the needs derived from an existing situation. These statements appear in a letter to a state library officer, and while they were written in specific response and reaction to a long-range plan for library service in a specific state, they have application in suggesting in a more general way, means of connecting objectives with goals, and goals with the needs from which they derive:

1. What are the needs of the people of _____ which can and should be served by a _____ library system?
2. What is the extent of the needs, i.e., who are the relevant populations involved? Where are they? And how many people are involved?
3. Can the problem be dealt with within the existing institutional framework, and if not, what changes need to be made to adequately serve these populations? And finally,
4. How critical is each identified need? In other words, what is the cost of meeting the need compared to the cost of ignoring it? . . . The point is that a clear statement of how much change is necessary is crucial to sound planning.[12]

In a letter to another state library officer, Robbins raised the following questions:

1. What is the source of these objectives (goals, targets)? What do these objectives represent? In other words, where did these objectives come from? Are they the result of meaningful assessment of the needs of the people of _____, or are they the policy decisions of a small group of individuals?
2. What are the priorities of your objectives? Are some more important than others, and if so, why (e.g., a particular objective has strong legislative support, etc.)? Can you identify the most critical objectives (i.e., the ones which address the most pressing needs)?
3. What do these objectives mean in light of your present situation? For example, are the programs which you specify as targets presently ongoing, in preparation, or still at the planning stage?
4. What are the temporal aspects of your plan? Are certain objectives to be sequenced or are all to be pursued at the same time?
5. How will you know when an objective has been realized?
6. How will you monitor the plan's success over time? Can you specify

12. David D. Thompson, ed., *Planning and Evaluation for Statewide Library Development: New Directions* (Columbus: Ohio State Univ. Faculty of Educational Development, 1972), p. 254.

certain benchmarks and/or timetables which you would consider to be successful implementation?[13]

STAFF AND COMMUNITY INVOLVEMENT

Ralph Conant points out the very real need for libraries to involve representatives from government, industry, business, and the professions, as well as all levels of the community, in making an assessment of societal needs. A serious concern with major problems can create a new image for the profession and involve the community in a vital understanding of what libraries can mean to the entire society.[14]

Barbara Conroy reinforces the concept of community involvement in assessing and establishing goals:

> The survival of the public library, as such, is presently in jeopardy. As a social institution, its function is to provide for the informational needs within its community. Presently, it is often found wanting in meeting this function. As a service agency, it is responsible to its clients. In the most dormant instances, its performance of this function is being ignored or by-passed. In the most alive instances, libraries and librarians are being asked to look to new roles and new patterns of service in the community.
>
> In theory, the library's clients include the entire spectrum of individuals and groups in the community. In actual practice . . . utilization of library services is often selective, due to the method by which library services are delivered or due to the lack of community awareness of or responsiveness to the services offered. . . . Access to information, having it and using it, is a strong element of power for individuals and groups. . . . The realization that having information is vital to what people want and need to do is a growing one. That realization translates into alternative means of getting information if public library services do not meet those needs. Some of the current alternatives include hotlines, government information centers, business reference services, etc. However they get it, citizens need information with which to make decisions in meeting their personal, career and civic responsibilities. . . .
>
> Most fundamentally, successful outreach programs are done by the librarian *with* the community, not by the librarian *for* the community. In this changing world, librarians need to . . . develop the necessary abilities and attitudes for outreach librarianship. Libraries need to build policies and programs which are closely related to community needs and which incorporate community involvement in new ways. The

13. Ibid., p. 265-66.
14. Dr. Ralph W. Conant, President, Southwest Center for Urban Research, in a speech presented before the American Library Association Conference, Las Vegas, Nevada, June 24, 1973.

community needs to change in relation to the library by actively being involved in the planning and use of library services.[15]

A Strategy for Public Library Change also calls attention to the critical need in librarianship for learning how to "set goals *with,* not *for* users."[16] This is an area in which librarians can learn much from the educators who have developed or adapted effective techniques for community involvement.

The Lang and Rose report on "Educational Goals and Objectives: A Model Program for Community Involvement" has been field tested with over three thousand educators in more than eighty workshops.[17] The experience has been found to be "worthwhile and nonthreatening" for community representatives, teachers, and students. Priority ranked goals are established and perceptions indicating the degrees to which programs meet goals are presented.

Another useful example is the approach used by the Program Development Center of Northern California. Although developed for elementary and secondary schools, their program can be applied to libraries of all types by direct terminology substitution, e.g., *library* for *school, users* for *pupils, librarians* for *teachers,* etc.

The program consists of a series of strategies whereby a school district may develop community-ranked educational goals and teacher-developed objectives. Provision is made for the involvement of members of the community, the professional staff, and students in:

1. ranking of educational goals in order of their importance
2. assessing how well current educational programs are meeting these goals, and
3. development of program level performance objectives by the professional staff designed to meet the priority-ranked goals.

In addition to providing for community, professional staff, and student involvement, this program allows a district or school to complete the program in a time span extending from six months to one year, without imposing unrealistic time requirements upon the participants, while at the same time providing the optimum amount of usable decision-making information. The cost factor (always an important element) is also kept at a minimal level.

It is important to note that this educational approach was developed in an attempt to provide a logical and orderly integration of the varied elements which contribute to increased accountability. The process begins with the ranking of priority goals by the community—moves

15. *Leadership for Change,* A Report of the Outreach Leadership Network, New England Center for Continuing Education (Durham: Univ. of New Hampshire, 1972), p. 4-6.

16. *Strategy for Public Library Change,* p. 52.

17. Carroll A. Lang and B. Keith Rose, "Community Involvement in Educational Accountability," *Phi Delta Kappan,* Oct. 1972, p. 80.

through the development of an instructional design which describes school efforts to achieve goals in terms of individual performance—and terminates in the allocation of resources to achieve predetermined objectives and to satisfy established goals.[18]

Other techniques are available and applicable. For example, Force Field Analysis (FFA) is a problem-solving scheme developed by Kurt Lewin, which can be used with children, adults, librarians, administrators, users, non-users, board members, in many combinations.[19] The purpose is to identify the various forces impinging upon a given condition, problem, or concern, and to seek solutions to negative forces. The number of participants is unlimited if the total group can be subdivided into groups of five to ten. For any given condition, there are both facilitating and inhibiting factors. For example, suppose a community is engaged in a program: "Things I want to say about and questions I want to ask about the goals established in the Illinois State Library's *Meeting the Challenge*." The group analysis would lead to the identification of both types of factors. Recommendations would be developed to maintain the facilitating factors and to minimize, if not eliminate, the inhibiting forces. Both positive and negative data are generated, which is particularly important in difficult situations. Techniques for ranking and weighting are used. Developing recommendations adds an important positive dimension to the process.

Although most of the examples quoted here have been concerned with agencies serving the general public, the applicability of the techniques and the necessity for the process of community—or clientele—involvement in determination of needs are self-evident for other types of libraries.

18. Northern California Program Development Center, *Educational Goals and Objectives: Administrator's Manual* (Distributed by Phi Delta Kappa, Bloomington, Ind., 1972).

19. Kurt Lewin, "Group Decision and Social Change," in Theodore M. Newcomb and Eugene L. Hartley, eds., *Readings in Social Psychology* (New York: Holt, 1952), p. 459-73.

Chapter 3

PROGRAMS TO MEET OBJECTIVES

Thus far there has been discussion of the identification of a library's central purpose, goals, and objectives. But, again, it is necessary to go back a step to consider the establishment of the library itself and its role in relationship to other libraries and other types of agencies in the community.

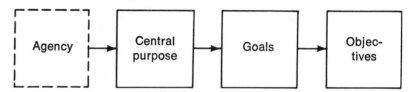

At the time a particular agency is created or selected to meet previously identified societal needs, there must be recognition of other traditional and nontraditional agencies designed to meet these needs.

Let us assume, for example, that through enlightened and successful techniques of community involvement in a needs assessment program the following needs have been identified: (1) information, (2) education, and (3) recreation. Librarianship has developed as one of society's answers to an acknowledged pattern of informational needs. It is seen as the ally and partner of the school; the tool for the individual citizen's educational and social progress; and as a link in conserving cultural patterns of succeeding generations.

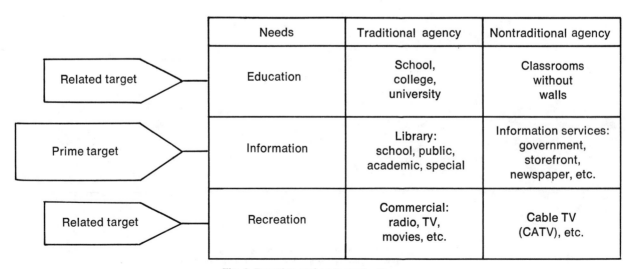

Fig. 3. Function and agency clusters

It is obvious, even from a quick look at figure 3, that the library's central role involves the three areas and indicates a close relationship among traditional and nontraditional agencies alike. It is equally obvious that libraries may be repeating poorly what others can do better or as well, or not doing what is being neglected by everyone and should be done.

To be efficient and effective the library must know, beyond the level of the superficial and the cursory, what all the related agencies in the community are doing. Not only should this knowledge be accurate and comprehensive but these other agencies should have the same depth of knowledge and appreciation of what the library is doing. This heightened consciousness calls for more effective interaction among the community's information-education-recreation agencies. This is a demanding responsibility. It is also an extremely productive area of study. The interaction among the various elements of community leadership will reinforce, support, and extend the usefulness of each.

Having established or identified an agency as a means for the gratification of human needs, and having specified the agency's central purpose, goals, and objectives, the next sequential steps are in the area of implementation. Implementation, most simply defined, is "carrying out, doing, or fulfilling." Goals and objectives are implemented through the development of subsystems, or clusters of actions or steps, which herein are called *programs*.

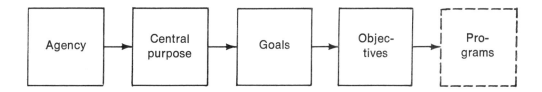

Programs follow rather than precede goals and objectives. Programs are, or should be, the outgrowth of two broad questions:

1. What services and resources are required to implement our objectives?
2. How successful are our current services and resources in implementing our objectives?

Synonymous with the use of the term *programs* is the term *requirements,* as used by the authors of *Libraries at Large:*

> It is widely accepted that people have needs for library services; i.e., access to books, serials, reports, and other library materials, and/or the information contained in them. Satisfying those needs imposes requirements for the design, construction, operation, and evolution of library systems. Requirements, in system-design terminology, are formal statements describing functions that need to be performed to allow a specific set of objectives to be met. There are several categories of library users, whose needs differ greatly from one to another. . . . These

needs, in turn, imply several kinds of requirements for different kinds of library services.[1]

1. Douglas M. Knight and E. Shepley Nourse, eds., *Libraries at Large* (New York: Bowker, 1969; © 1969 by Duke University), p. 288-89.

User Service Requirements
1. Browsing access to library materials
2. Searching access via catalogs, indexes, and other reference tools
3. Question-answering service
4. Directive service for reference or referral
5. Reading guidance
6. Instruction in use of catalogs, indexes, and other reference tools
7. Reading, viewing, and listening facilities
8. Bibliographic compilation
9. Reproduction of materials (copying facilities)
10. Loan and interlibrary loan
11. Discussion groups
12. Storytelling and readings to users
13. Paging and other delivery services (e.g., bookmobiles).

Internal Operational Requirements

1. Acquisition of materials:
   a. Selection and bibliographic checking
   b. Gifts and exchanges
   c. Ordering and accounting
   d. Receiving and disbursing

2. Cataloging:
   a. Bibliographic checking
   b. Descriptive cataloging
   c. Classification and subject cataloging
   d. Marking and labeling

3. Storage:
   a. Shelving and other storage media
   b. Preservation and protection
   c. Locating and arranging
   d. Retrieval and replacement

4. Management:
   a. Planning, organizing, supervising, delegating
   b. Coordinating, reporting, budgeting
   c. Personnel selection and training
   d. Record-keeping and statistics

Fig. 4. Typical requirements for direct service to library users and internal operational requirements

Libraries at Large goes on to identify three related types of requirements:

1. requirements for direct service to users
2. internal operational requirements, essential for rendering direct service in a library
3. external operational requirements; i.e., requirements for interfacing with external systems of libraries and other information-handling organizations.[2]

Figure 4 illustrates typical requirements for direct service to users and internal operational requirements.[3]

In the case study of the organization and staffing of the libraries of Columbia University sponsored by the Association of Research Libraries, three major operating units were recommended, each of which would have responsibility for certain programs.[4] These are shown in figure 5.

2. Ibid., p. 289.
3. Ibid, p. 294.
4. Booz, Allen & Hamilton, Inc., *Organization and Staffing of the Libraries of Columbia University: A Summary of the Case Study* (Washington, D.C.: Assn. of Research Libraries, 1972), p. 7.

Resources Group will comprise primarily professional staff, will work primarily with faculty and researchers, and will . . .

Plan and carry out programs and services of:
Collection development and preservation
In-depth reference and research assistance
Classroom instruction assistance and participation
Original cataloging

Services Group will include a few professional staff members and many technical and support staff members, will serve library users on a day-to-day basis, and will . . .

Operate service centers (bringing together existing small service units) that will:
Serve library users' immediate needs
Provide first-line information and referral services
Provide self-service access to library collections
Provide ready reference assistance

Support Group will include a few professional staff members and many technical and support staff members, and will . . .

Provide support services to the Services Group and the Resources Group, including:
Acquisition of library materials
Production of bibliographic records
Processing of library materials
Photographic services
Systems analysis
Computer services
Facilities management and security
Fiscal control

Fig. 5. Major operating units recommended

The libraries of the University of California, through a series of committees and task forces during 1969-71, developed a set of subsystems and modules, comprising and defining the total library system for the University as shown in figure 6, along with a flow chart showing the primary interrelationships among the subsystems (see figure 7).[5]

Programs in turn can be broken down into *functions, activities,* or what the University of California study calls *modules:*

1.0 COLLECTION DEVELOPMENT SUBSYSTEM
1.1 *Collection Information Module*
  Maintains and analyzes statistics on collection size and development. Monitors collection changes as a function of time, subjects, types of material, volume of material, and location. Produces analytical reports.
1.2 *Collection Planning Module*
  Projects required collection development needs. Sets collection policy. Develops budget requests. Manages book funds. Determines amounts for standing orders, approval plans, retrospective buying, and subject areas.
1.3 *Library Materials Selection Module*
  Selects library material. Authorizes or declines all requests for items requested by faculty, staff, or students (whether submitted on a request card, a marked list, a dealer's catalog, or other means). Obtains appropriate committee approvals where necessary.
1.4 *Offerings Evaluation Module*
  Evaluates and authorizes purchase of bulk purchases. Sets up standing order plans. Continues to evaluate plans. Evaluates titles in bulk purchases and on approval plans. Evaluates gifts and titles on gifts. Decides destination of duplicates. Evaluates exchange offers.

2.0 REQUEST SUBSYSTEM
2.1 *Request Handling Module*
  Prepares requests for entrance into the system. Entails channeling request to appropriate selection personnel. Sets up preliminary in-process record.
2.2 *Request Handling Services Module*
  Receives and processes requests for reserves. Transmits requests for material to be purchased. Transmits information for changing public holding records to show new location.[6]

Beginning with the identification of tasks, rather than following the sequence of central purpose, goals, objectives, and programs as advocated here, SERD arranged the tasks into nine "functional areas":

1. Administration
2. Selection and Acquisition

---

5. *Library System Definition: Functions and Interfaces* (Santa Barbara: Univ. of California, 1971), back cover and p. 3.
6. Ibid., p. 4.

```
1.0   COLLECTION-DEVELOPMENT SUBSYSTEM-(1.1) Collection Information,
      (1.2) Collection Planning, (1.3) Library Materials Selection,
      (1.4) Offerings Evaluation.
2.0   REQUEST SUBSYSTEM-(2.1) Request Handling, (2.2) Request
      Handling Services.
3.0   SOURCE SELECTION SUBSYSTEM-(3.1) Vendor Decision, (3.2)
      Vendor Performance Analysis.
4.0   BIBLIOGRAPHIC SEARCHING SUBSYSTEM-(4.1) Searching
5.0   BIBLIOGRAPHIC RECORD SUBSYSTEM-(5.1) Bibliographic Record,
      (5.2) Catalog Maintenance, (5.3)Bibliographic Authority
      Control.
6.0   ORDER SUBSYSTEM-(6.1) Surplus Control, (6.2) Order Initiation,
      (6.3)Claims Processing, (6.4)Receiving, (6.5)Invoice Process-
      ing, (6.6)Vendor File Maintenance, (6.7)Want List Processing.
7.0   ACCOUNTING SUBSYSTEM-(7.1)Book Fund Accounting,(7.2)Currency
      Conversion, (7.3)Administrative Accounting.
8.0   AUXILIARY SOURCE SUBSYSTEM-(8.1)Donor Registry Maintenance,
      (8.2)Exchange Program Control.
9.0   BOOK PREPARATION SUBSYSTEM-(9.1)Binding Control, (9.2)Book
      Labeling
10.0  PROCESS MONITORING SUBSYSTEM-(10.1)Cost Accounting, (10.2)
      In-Process Control.
11.0  STANDARD LOAN SUBSYSTEM-(11.1)Book Charging, (11.2)Book
      Discharging, (11.3)Holds and Recalls Processing, (11.4)
      Long Term Loan List Production, (11.5)Interlibrary Loan
      Control, (11.6)Patron Registry Maintenance, (11.7) Overdue
      Book Processing.
13.0  STACK CONTROL SUBSYSTEM-(13.1)Collection Accessibility, (13.2)
      Collection Inventory, (13.3)Stack Maintenance.
14.0  INFORMATION RETRIEVAL SUBSYSTEM-(14.1)Bibliography Prepar-
      ation, (14.2)Selective Dissemination of Information.
16.0  PATRON SERVICES SUBSYSTEM-(16.1)Information Guidance Services,
      (16.2)Patron Services.
17.0  SERVICES QUALITY CONTROL SUBSYSTEM-(17.1)Faculty Liason,
      (17.2)Patron Relations, (17.3)Service Planning, (17.4)
      Patron Use Analysis.
18.0  FISCAL SUBSYSTEM-(18.1)Budget Development, (18.2)Fiscal
      Resource Utilization Analysis, (18.3)Funding Source Report-
      ing, (18.4)Salary Savings Projections.
19.0  PERSONNEL SUBSYSTEM-(19.1)Timekeeping, (19.2)Personnel
      Information, (19.3)Desk Scheduling, (19.4)Staffing Needs
      Projection, (19.5)Recruitment Planning, (19.6)Personnel
      Training.
20.0  EQUIPMENT & SUPPLIES SUBSYSTEM-(20.1)Equipment Information,
      (20.2)Equipment Selection, (20.3)Supplies Inventory.
21.0  PHYSICAL PLANT & FACILITIES SUBSYSTEM-(21.1)Building Plan-
      ning, (21.2)Space Utilization, (21.3)Work Flow Analysis,
      (21.4)Security Control.
22.0  LIBRARY DOCUMENT SUBSYSTEM-(22.1)Forms Control and Design,
      (22.2)Publications Planning and Control, (22.3)Documents
      Control, (22.4)Mail Processing.
24.0  ORGANIZATION & POLICY SUBSYSTEM-(24.1)Academic Plans Analysis,
      (24.2)Library Legislation Reporting, (24.3)Organization
      Analysis Procedure, (24.4)Administrative Information Control.
```

Fig. 6. The total system

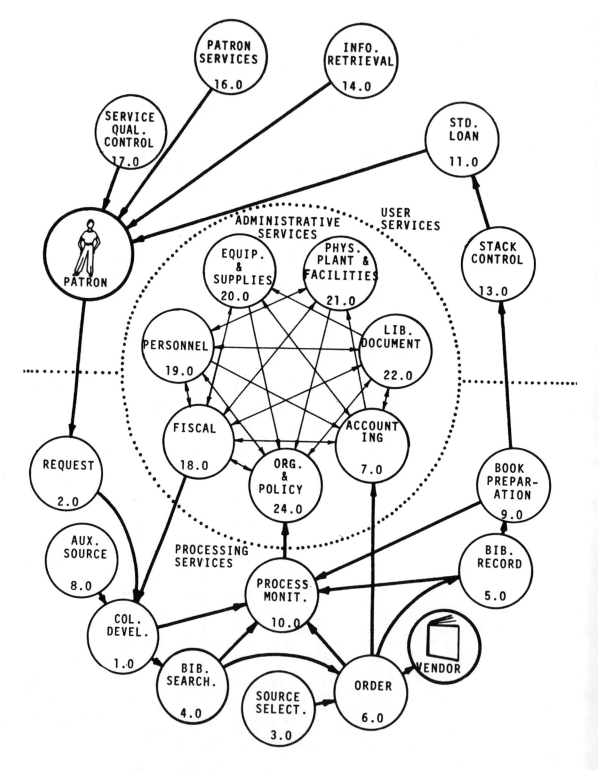

Fig. 7. Subsystem interrelationships

3. Cataloging and Processing
4. Registration and Circulation
5. Reference Services
6. Patron Services
   a. Children's Services
   b. Adult Services
   c. Special Group Services
   d. Special Activities
7. Collection Maintenance
8. Facility Maintenance
9. Miscellaneous.

And, following a similar process in Phases II and III of the project, the tasks included here in chapter 6 are arranged into eight subsystems:

1. Collection Development
2. Collection Organization
3. Collection Preparation and Maintenance
4. Collection Storage and Retrieval
5. Circulation
6. Collection Interpretation and Use
7. Management
8. Staff Development.

Thus, approaching from either direction, it can be seen that *tasks,* as defined in chapter 1, represent the next step in our systems process.

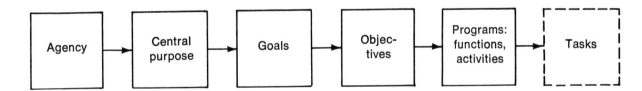

And it is from tasks, through the process described in chapter 1, that *jobs* are structured.

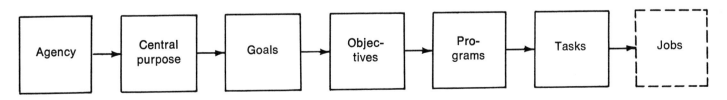

A fundamental question might be asked, "Do programs determine jobs, or do jobs determine programs?" When agencies have lost sight of their objectives, goals, and central purpose, there is a high probability that jobs are determining programs rather than the other way around. If this is the case, to paraphrase Toffler (who was writing about schools), ". . . our [libraries] face backward toward a dying system, rather than forward to the emerging new society. . . ."[7] As we look forward to the emergence of new societal needs, the organizational structure of a library currently in force must not be confused with programs designed to meet needs.

7. Alvin Toffler, *Future Shock* (New York: Random House, 1970), p. 354.

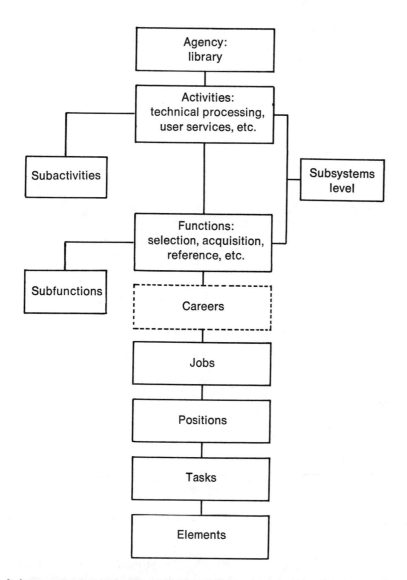

Fig. 8. A generalized model widely prevalent in libraries

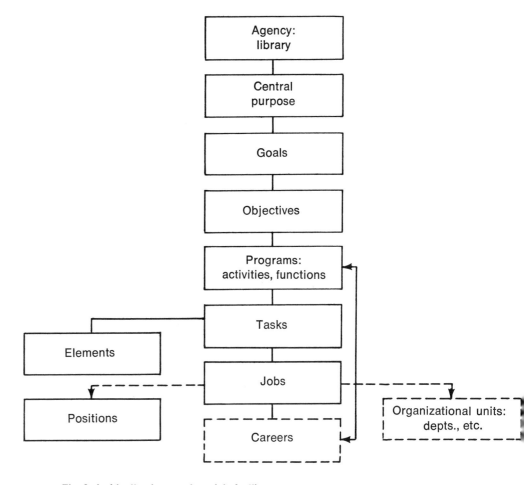

Fig. 9. An idealized general model of a library

A library (or any other agency) is too often viewed in the manner shown in figure 8. When libraries are viewed this way, activities, functions, or even programs tend to become equated with organizational structure in the form of departments or other administrative units. Accordingly, jobs (and thus positions and eventually careers) become polarized around these units, with little thought given to changing objectives, goals, and societal needs. Career goals become agency goals; the preservation of traditional functions becomes twisted into appropriate goal jargon; societal needs get lost in the polarization of careers around the sacred departments; creative staff people accept rigidity as a concomitant of security.

Figure 9, in contrast, represents an idealized model which probably few libraries have achieved. The idealized model stresses the importance of central purpose, goals, objectives, and programs in a definite sequential order. It also shows tasks emerging from programs, and careers in a more fluid state related to programs rather than rigidly linked with jobs or organizational units.

Many practical problems arise from the concepts shown in figure 9, particularly since most libraries are ongoing organizations involving a mix of human, material, and fiscal resources operating in social environments that vary widely in capacity to initiate or adapt to change. The ability to reorganize becomes critical if agencies are going to be able to change programs to meet changing societal needs. This implies a flexibility of approach to the work which is performed, which can best be expressed in the paradigm shown in figure 10.

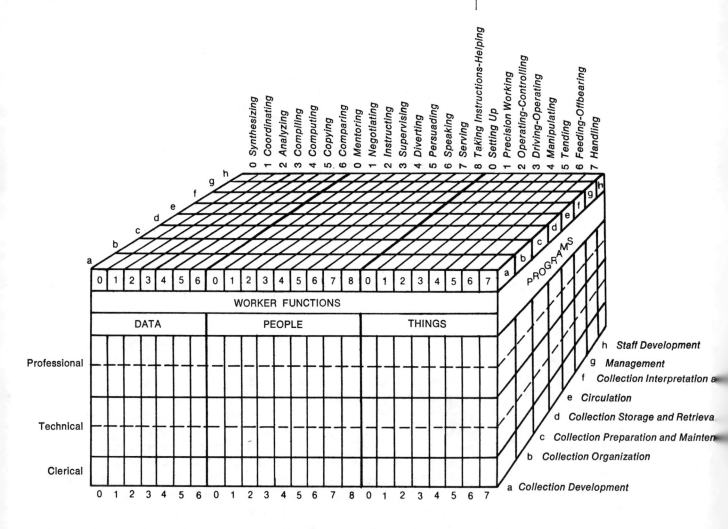

Fig. 10. A paradigm for the correlation of programs, worker functions, and categories of personnel

The programs used in the paradigm are those used in chapter 6 here; the worker functions are those defined by the U.S. Department of Labor (Appendix B); and the categories of personnel are based on the ALA policy statement, *Library Education and Manpower* (Appendix D). The correlation of the three can thus be visualized, and specific tasks or jobs can be reevaluated in terms of changing needs, central purpose, goals, and objectives.

Chapter 4

HUMAN RELATIONS MANAGEMENT

Just as task analysis and job design cannot be approached except in terms of the organizational goals and objectives to be achieved, so also can they not be approached without proper understanding of the goals and motivations of the individuals, the human beings, who perform the work.

For a very long time in classical management theory, specialization was accepted as the primary organizing principle, and Max Weber described bureaucracy as the most efficient form of social organization ever developed.[1] The concentration of skills in a highly stratified personnel structure has an obvious economic efficiency, and its appeal is enlarged when certain high level skills are hard to obtain. Within the last twenty-five years, however, many students of management have questioned whether this approach, based implicitly on the assumption that the content and structure of jobs is determined by the requirements of the production process, is indeed the most productive.

As long ago as 1950, Peter Drucker began to argue that the use of the worker as a single-purpose tool is poor engineering and a waste of human resources.[2]

Chris Argyris pointed out:

> To the extent that individuals who are hired to become agents of organizations are predisposed to maturity, they will want to express needs and predispositions related to the adult end of each specific developmental continuum. Theoretically, this means that healthy adults will tend to obtain optimum personality expression while at work if they are provided with jobs which permit them to be more active than passive; more independent than dependent; to have longer rather than shorter time perspectives; to occupy higher positions than their peers; to have control over their world; and to express many of their deeper, more important abilities.

> [Whereas,] If the principles of formal organization are used as ideally defined, employees will tend to work in an environment where (1) they are provided minimal control over their workaday world, (2) they are expected to be passive, dependent, and subordinate, (3) they are expected to have a short time perspective, (4) they are induced to perfect and value the frequent use of a few skin-surface shallow abilities, and

---

1. *The Theory of Social and Economic Organization,* tr. and ed. by A. M. Henderson and Talcott Parsons (New York: Oxford, 1947).
2. *The New Society* (New York: Harper, 1950).

(5) they are expected to produce under conditions leading to psychological failure.

> All these characteristics are incongruent to the ones *healthy* human beings are postulated to desire . . . . This incongruency increases as (1) the employees are of increasing maturity, (2) the formal structure is made more clear-cut and logically tight for maximum formal organizational effectiveness, (3) as one goes down the line of command, and (4) as jobs become more and more mechanized.[3]

Much is being written currently about what Drucker called "managing the educated."[4] Maslow's hierarchy of needs, treated at length in chapter 2, makes very clear why today the traditional incentives of salary and security are no longer motivating factors for a large portion of the working population.[5] Esteem needs and, more importantly, the need for self-actualization are now becoming dominant for a higher percentage of the work force.

On the basis of these theories,

> In contrast with [the] *process-centered* approach, another concept of job design has developed in recent years—the *worker-centered* approach, which emphasizes the participation of the worker in certain areas of decision making as a way of giving meaning to the work situation. Representative of this approach . . . [is] *job enlargement,* . . . in which the job is specified in such a manner that the worker performs a longer sequence or a greater variety of operations. . . .

> [Another] approach . . . *combines* the process-centered and worker-centered approaches. In *job rotation* . . . the operator is assigned a series of jobs to be performed in rotated order where the basic specifications cannot be altered for one reason or another.[6]

Applications of these approaches are not difficult to achieve in libraries. Numbers of libraries now assign professional staff on a subject basis, with full responsibility for acquisition and cataloging as well as reference service within an area. An effective use of rotation can be achieved by assigning circulation staff to work alternately on overdues, the charge desk, reserves, and registration, so that variety lightens the monotony in any one set of tasks.

In 1960 Douglas McGregor warned:

> What sometimes appear to be new strategies—decentralization, management by objectives, consultative supervision, "democratic" leadership—are usually but old wine in new bottles, because the

---

3. *Personality and Organization* (New York: Harper, 1957), p. 53, 66.
4. In Dan H. Fenn, ed., *Management's Mission in a New Society* (New York: McGraw-Hill, 1956), p. 163-78.
5. Maslow, *Motivation and Personality.*
6. Louis E. Davis, "Job Design and Productivity: A New Approach," *Personnel,* Mar. 1957, p. 420-21.

procedures developed to implement them are derived from the same inadequate assumptions about human nature.[7]

Asserting that "behind every managerial decision or action are assumptions about human nature and human behavior," he points out that Theory X, the traditional view of direction and control, is based on assumptions which include:

1. The average human being has an inherent dislike of work and will avoid it if he can . . . .
2. Because of this human characteristic of dislike of work, most people must be coerced, controlled, directed, threatened with punishment to get them to put forth adequate effort toward the achievement of organizational objectives . . . .
3. The average human being prefers to be directed, wishes to avoid responsibility, has relatively little ambition, wants security above all . . . .[8]

He offers in contrast Theory Y, based on the assumptions that:

1. The expenditure of physical and mental effort in work is as natural as play or rest . . . .
2. External control and the threat of punishment are not the only means for bringing about effort toward organizational objectives. Man will exercise self-direction and self-control in the service of objectives to which he is committed . . . .
3. Commitment to objectives is a function of the rewards associated with their achievement . . . .
4. The average human being learns, under proper conditions, not only to accept but to seek responsibility . . . .
5. The capacity to exercise a relatively high degree of imagination, ingenuity, and creativity in the solution of organizational problems is widely, not narrowly, distributed in the population . . . .[9]

Assumptions such as these will obviously lead to a different form of job design and a different form of organization from the one admired by Weber. As Mason Haire expressed it, "in traditional theory the organization structure was the independent variable, behavior the dependent; the behaviorists reversed this."[10]

As Louis Davis suggests, there undoubtedly needs to be a third approach to job design—"the *job-centered* approach—which goes beyond the process-

7. Douglas McGregor, *The Human Side of Enterprise* (New York: McGraw-Hill, 1960), p. 42.

8. Ibid., p. 33-34.

9. Ibid., p. 47-48.

10. Mason Haire, Alfred P. Sloan Professor of Management, Massachusetts Institute of Technology, in a paper presented at the University of Chicago Graduate Library School Conference, April 9, 1973.

centered and worker-centered approaches. The job-centered approach operates on the premise that a job cannot be adequately designed without taking into account all three of these basic variables—process, worker, and organization—as well as the variables arising from their interaction."[11]

11. Davis, "Job Design and Productivity," p. 429.

DIMENSIONS	CHARACTERISTICS	
	Static Organizations	Innovative Organizations
Structure	Rigid—much energy given to maintaining permanent departments, committees; reverence for tradition, constitution and by-laws. Hierarchical—adherence to chain of command. Roles defined narrowly. Property-bound.	Flexible—much use of temporary task forces; easy shifting of departmental lines; readiness to change constitution, depart from tradition. Multiple linkages based on functional collaboration. Roles defined broadly. Property-mobile.
Atmosphere	Task-centered, impersonal. Cold, formal, reserved. Suspicious.	People-centered, caring. Warm, informal, intimate. Trusting.
Management Philosophy and Attitudes	Function of management is to control personnel through coercive power. Cautious—low risk-taking. Attitude toward errors: to be avoided. Emphasis on personnel selection. Self-sufficiency—closed system regarding sharing resources. Emphasis on conserving resources. Low tolerance for ambiguity.	Function of management is to release the energy of personnel; power is used supportively. Experimental—high risk-taking. Attitude toward errors: to be learned from. Emphasis on personnel development. Interdependency—open system regarding sharing resources. Emphasis on developing and using resources. High tolerance for ambiguity.
Decision-making and Policy-making	High participation at top, low at bottom. Clear distinction between policy-making and policy-execution. Decision-making by legal mechanisms. Decisions treated as final.	Relevant participation by all those affected. Collaborative policy-making and policy-execution. Decision-making by problem-solving. Decisions treated as hypotheses to be tested.
Communication	Restricted flow—constipated. One-way—downward. Feelings repressed or hidden.	Open flow—easy access. Multidirectional—up, down, sideways. Feelings expressed.

Fig. 11. Some characteristics of static vs. innovative organizations

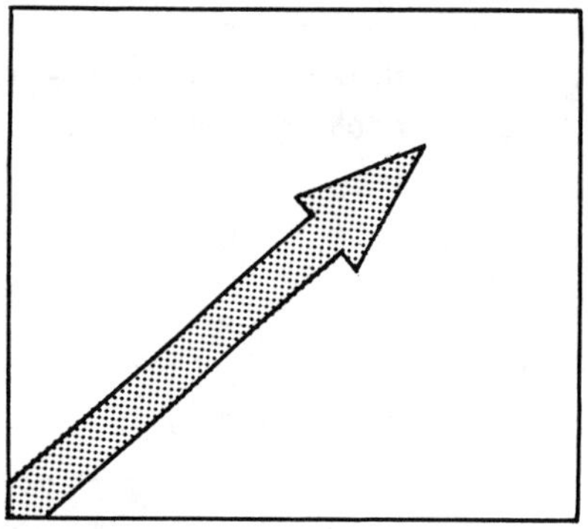

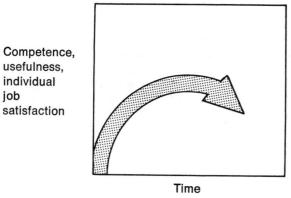

Fig. 12. (Ideal) An employee's competence, usefulness, and job satisfaction over a long period of time on the job

Fig. 13. (Actual) An employee's competence, usefulness, and job satisfaction over a long period of time on the job

Some form of participatory (democratic) management is recommended for all of the processes described in our model. When staff members at all levels become involved in assesssing community needs, determining central purposes, goals, objectives, and programs, there will be closer harmony between them and the agency in which they are employed. Agencies in which this occurs might be characterized as "innovative," in contrast with "rigid and static" agencies in which fiat, decree, and directives are the standard practice.

Knowles has developed a paradigm portraying some characteristics of static vs. innovative organizations (see figure 11).[12] It is almost universally hoped,

12. Malcolm S. Knowles, *The Modern Practice of Adult Education: Andragogy versus Pedagogy* (New York: Association Pr., 1970), p. 62.

by employers and employees alike, that over a period of time an employee's competency, effectiveness, and personal job satisfaction will continue to grow as shown in figure 12. However, in all too many cases, over a period of time the competency, effectiveness, usefulness to the agency, and personal satisfaction on a job falls off rather sharply, as shown in figure 13. To avoid the downward curve shown in figure 13 requires: (1) creative job design, based on the goals of the individual as well as those of the organization; (2) involvement of the individual in determining the organization's purpose, goals, objectives, and programs; and (3) a flexible career movement within the agency as programs change and individuals develop.

Chapter 5

THE COMPLETED MODEL

Having come through the steps in the systems approach shown in figure 14, it should be noted that the lowercase letters indicate the relationship to the original Wiley and Fine model (see figure 1).

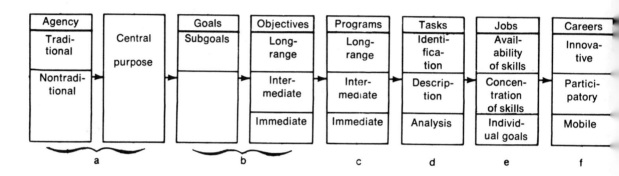

Fig. 14. Systems process

It is now necessary to add to the model four parameters—four activities which must constantly, continuously be repeated for every step included in the model. Together they form a holistic structure within which any series of sequential steps (designated X for purposes of illustration in figure 15) can be studied.

These activities are called *systemic* because each applies to the system as a whole, and, as the arrows in figure 15 indicate, each one of the four also applies to each of the others.

The first of these parameters is *needs assessment,* already treated fully in chapter 2.

The second, *evaluation,* is "the process of determining the kinds of decisions that have to be made and selecting, collecting, and interpreting the information needed in making these decisions."[1] An extremely pertinent document for librarians concerned with evaluation is the study produced by the former Evaluation Center at Ohio State University.

> During the period 1971-72, the Center engaged in a 12-month program, sponsored by the Division of Library Programs in the Bureau of Libraries and Educational Technology in the U.S. Office of Education, to train heads of state library administrative agencies and Library

1. Stephen B. Klein, *Evaluation Workshop I: Participants' Notebook* (Monterey, Calif.: CTB/McGraw-Hill, 1971), p. A-2.

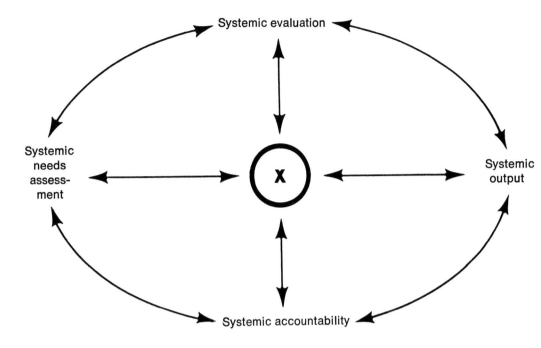

Fig. 15. Parameters of systems model

Services and Construction Act planners in each state in the concepts, methods, and procedures of evaluation and planning .The training program focused directly upon the charge that the U.S. Office of Education gave to each State Library Agency for the implementation of long-range planning processes as required by the Library Services and Construction Amendment of 1970.[2]

The third parameter, *output,* derives from a basic definition of a system as:

> . . . having an input, a process, and an output. A system spans time and connotes some change in state occurring between the input and output (many times referred to as the process).[3]

A library can be thought of as generating products, services, or ideas (knowledge). The input-process-output concept for a library is diagrammed in figure 16.[4]

Stufflebeam presents a case for the CIPP model (Context, Input, Process, Product) as one evaluation approach which is in harmony with the concept presented here of systemic evaluation:

2. Thompson, *Planning and Evaluation for Statewide Library Development,* p. ix.
3. William Gephart, ed., *Educational Evaluation and Decision Making,* Phi Delta Kappa, National Study Committee on Evaluation (Itasca, Ill.: F. E. Peacock, 1971), p. 124-25.
4. Ibid., p. 125 (adapted from).

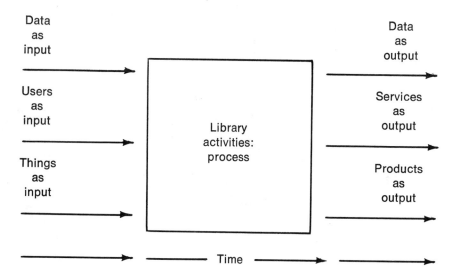

Fig. 16. Library input-process-output chart

The traditional view of program development includes four main steps:

1. Setting up objectives
2. Structuring a program to achieve the objectives
3. Implementation of the program
4. Evaluation of the results.

Clearly this has been a faulty conception. To wait until a program has been carried through before it is evaluated is not a reasonable decision; in addition to evaluating the *results,* it is also essential to evaluate the objectives, the program design, and the process of carrying through the program design. Moreover, the evaluation process itself must be systematic.[5]

The five-year plan (1971-76) of the State Library of Pennsylvania (figure 17) provides a good example of systemic CIPP evaluation.[6]

5. Daniel L. Stufflebeam, "The CIPP Model of Evaluation," in *Planning and Evaluation for Statewide Library Development,* p. 34.

6. Pennsylvania Department of Education, State Library of Pennsylvania, *A Five-Year Plan: Pennsylvania Library Development, 1971-76,* p. 43.

	CONTEXT EVALUATION	INPUT EVALUATION	PROCESS EVALUATION	PRODUCT EVALUATION
OBJECTIVE	To define the operating context, to identify and assess needs and opportunities in the context, and to diagnose problems underlying the needs and opportunities.	To identify and assess system capabilities, available input strategies, and designs for implementing the strategies.	To identify or predict, in process, defects in the procedural design or its implementation; to provide information for the preprogrammed decisions; and to maintain a record of procedural events and activities.	To relate outcome information to objectives and to context, input, and process information.
METHOD	By describing the context; by comparing actual and intended inputs and outputs; by comparing probable and possible system performance; and by analyzing possible causes of discrepancies between actualities and intentions.	By describing and analyzing available human and material resources, solution strategies, and procedural designs for relevance, feasibility, and economy in the course of action to be taken.	By monitoring the activity's potential procedural barriers and remaining alert to unanticipated ones, by obtaining specified information for programmed decisions, and by describing the actual process.	By defining operationally and measuring criteria associated with the objectives, by comparing these measurements with predetermined standards or comparative bases, and by interpreting the outcomes in terms of recorded context, input, and process information.
RELATION TO DECISION-MAKING IN THE CHANGE PROCESS	For deciding upon the setting to be served, the goals associated with meeting needs or using opportunities, and the objectives associated with solving problems, i.e., for planning needed changes.	For selecting sources of support, solution strategies, and procedural designs, i.e., for structuring change activities.	For implementing and refining the program design, and procedure, i.e., for effecting process control.	For deciding to continue, terminate, modify, or refocus a change activity, and for linking the activity to other major phases of the change process, i.e., for recycling change activities.

Fig. 17. Four types of evaluation

Systemic accountability is the fourth parameter in the model. *Systemic* again refers to the system as a whole. *Accountability* means:

Who is responsible to whom?
For what?
How?
By whose standards?
Within what time frame?
With what consequences?[7]

7. Definition used by Professor Albert F. Stahl, College of Education, Wayne State University, Detroit, Mich., April 1973.

Accountability must be thought of as a "top down" as well as a "bottom up" process. We are accountable for what we do or do not do with needs assessment, evaluation, output, as well as every step within the framework of our model. This includes central purpose, goals, objectives, programs, tasks, jobs, and careers.

Thus the model is now complete and may be seen as a whole in figure 18.

The process which has been described here is lengthy and complex. But there are no shortcuts—no "instant needs assessment" or "instant goal setting" or "instant task analysis."

The systems approach to task analysis is not a panacea. It is a tool. It will not in itself achieve more effective utilization of personnel, but it establishes a basis for it. It also provides an accurate and objective basis for the recruitment and selection of staff, the determination of their educational preparation and in-service training needs, the development of performance standards, and the systematic evaluation of performance. And, in relating the work performed by each individual to the overall goals of the agency, it not only reveals clearer lines for staff growth and development but simultaneously, for these reasons, improves morale and performance.

As Peter Drucker has said, the primary problem facing administrators and managers today lies in the intelligent establishment of organizational objectives, the recognition and understanding of individual career objectives, and the reconciliation or focusing of the two into mutually sought after and desirable goals.

The authors believe that the systems approach advocated here, difficult though it may be, is a means of solving this primary problem.

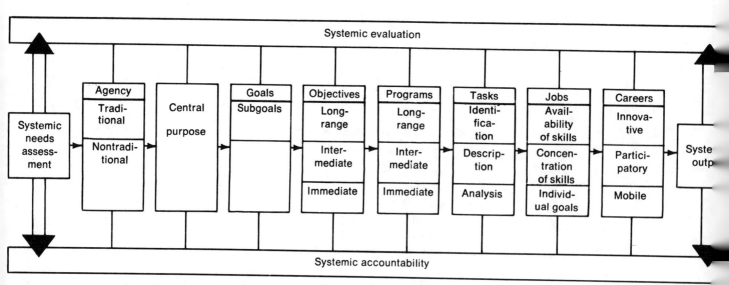

Fig. 18. A systems approach to personnel utilization in libraries

Chapter 6

TASK LIST

The following list of functions and tasks is derived from the 1,615 tasks originally identified by SERD in Phase I of ILTAP. Each of them occurred in one or more of the eighteen Illinois libraries included in the study (see Foreword). Each was evaluated on the SERD scales (Appendix A), and reevaluated as to its placement in position categories by one of the three Phase II consultants. (See Appendix E for methodology.) This placement was rereviewed in Phase III by the consultants, the advisory committee of ILTAP, and the participants in the three state library association workshops.

Even so, the resulting list can only be considered a suggestive arrangement —not in any sense of the word a model. Although the methodology is applicable in any type of library, of any size, the evaluation and placement of tasks here was based on the general size of the libraries included in the study. This had a significant effect on the placement by level of some functions. For example, "Controls record of all serials acquired by the library" (1-T-5) was allocated here at the Technical level. There are libraries in which this function might be allocated at a very high professional level, and others in which it could be considered clerical.

Also, because the tasks occurred in eighteen different libraries, not within a single integrated system, they cannot be counted on to mesh together into an articulated whole. For the same reason, various methods of performing the work are intermingled in numbers of the tasks described. Particularly at the clerical level, machine and manual methods are intermixed as they occurred in the practices of the eighteen libraries.

Not all the tasks listed here will be performed in your library; nor can it be assumed that all the tasks performed in your library are included here. Although reviewed by the consultants, committee, and the workshop participants for significant omissions, the list was not circulated to other libraries for detailed review of this kind. Thus, the nature of the libraries included is again an influential factor. As an example, the Collection Preparation and Maintenance subsystem places relatively little emphasis on preservation from the point of view of a research library, but is more concerned with the preparation of materials for circulation.

Often, the specific application must be derived from a quite broad statement of a function. For example, "Coordinates selection of materials with needs and resources of other appropriate libraries and organizations" (1-P-2) covers an almost infinite variety of complex tasks performed in school, public, academic, and special libraries. But since the purpose of this study is to demonstrate a methodology, it was identified as a professional function without further elaboration.

In this connection, also, such words as *user, clientele, library, materials* have been given the broadest possible interpretation. (See special glossary accompanying the list.)

The tasks are arranged in eight major subsystems or programs:

1. Collection Development
2. Collection Organization
3. Collection Preparation and Maintenance
4. Collection Storage and Retrieval
5. Circulation
6. Collection Interpretation and Use
7. Management
8. Staff Development.

This is purely a functional arrangement, not to be confused with the organization structure of a library. For example, a librarian who works in a public service unit of a library will undoubtedly perform certain functions concerned with collection development. Similarly, the professional functions and tasks in the Personnel and Public Relations modules of the Management program cut across the line/staff relationships involved in these areas to include tasks performed by both specialists and librarians. In other words, the tasks in any given program are not necessarily assigned to a given position or organizational unit, and conversely, the tasks comprising any individual position may be drawn from a number of programs. This permits and emphasizes the flexibility of utilization discussed in chapter 3.

Within each program, the tasks are arranged by three categories of personnel: (1) Professional, (2) Technical, and (3) Clerical. In Phase II, the three consultants attempted to allocate the tasks to all nine of the categories established in the ALA policy statement, *Library Education and Manpower* (Appendix D). In Phase III, two of the categories, Senior Librarian and Senior Specialist, were eliminated early in the consolidation of the list, since this kind of distinction by level can only be done in terms of the organization structure and size of the library unit or system in which the tasks occur. Similarly, many of the tasks listed in the several Professional modules of the Management subsystem could be assigned to either Librarians or Specialists, again depending on the organization structure, size, and point of view of the library in which they occur. The Specialist category is a much needed one, and it is important to retain the distinction between it and the Librarian, but this can be done only in given organizations, not in a study of this type.

The Library Associate/Associate Specialist categories were not used here simply because, in a task analysis approach, there were almost no tasks that could appropriately be assigned to this level. Again, this is an extremely useful category of *personnel,* but the *tasks* are essentially professional and the bachelor's degree person performing them is, more often than not, working in a trainee capacity. The Technical Assistant/Library Technical Assistant categories were simply merged as not being of sufficient distinction in view of the consolidation in the other categories.

Within categories the tasks are arranged, to the extent feasible, in sequential (i.e., chronological or functional) order; they are not in the order of difficulty. They are codified in the following manner for identification and access:

1. First arabic number = program or subsystem
2. Capital letter = personnel category
3. Lowercase letter = module within a program
4. Second whole arabic number = function
5. Decimal arabic number = task.

Thus: 5-C-b-9.1 identifies the task, "Files circulation cards by call number," in the Circulation subsystem, Clerical category, Circulation module, under the function "Keeps circulation records."

There is no relationship between the numbering of the tasks in the three respective categories of personnel. In other words, Task 1-P-1 is not necessarily supported by Task 1-T-1 or 1-C-1. Although the grouping of tasks within any subsystem or module by category of personnel provides a useful basis for comparison, the comparison should not be made on a literal across-the-page reading of individual tasks or functions.

There are a number of useful purposes the list can serve:

1. It helps to define the nature of three distinct levels of work activity in libraries—professional, technical, and clerical. This can be useful in assigning work and developing positions in a given library organization, in interpreting these levels to hiring and budgetary authorities, and in developing and evaluating appropriate programs of educational preparation for the three levels. It also provides a base for realistic recruitment and for the development of performance measures and standards and the evaluation of staff performance.
2. It suggests a basis for evolving more clearly in individual library systems the interrelationships among the three levels, with development and clarification of appropriate career structures.
3. Perhaps most important of all, it is hoped that the compilation of such a list of tasks actually being performed will permit and encourage critical review and the asking, in individual libraries, of the questions: Should these tasks be performed? What is their contribution toward our agreed-upon goals and objectives? Should the tasks be performed in the manner described here (or as presently performed in our library)? Or is there a more effective methodology? A review of the tasks on which an agency's personnel *is* expending its time and talent is often the necessary first step toward determining how it *should* be expending them to achieve established goals in the most expeditious way.

This was something those involved in the project could not do because to be working in the abstract is to be without the goals of a given organization to provide direction. This is why you, in your own library, cannot just adopt this list as yours, but must adapt, identify other tasks growing out of the goals of your agency, and perhaps assign some tasks to different position categories.

This you do in the light of your own goals, your own evaluations, and your own arrangements of jobs, positions, and appropriate career structures.

To repeat: it is a complex and therefore costly process. But well done, it can more than pay for itself in the clearer view it provides of a library's personnel needs.

GLOSSARY FOR TASK LIST

Clientele Those served by the particular library: students, faculty, the public at large, children, or any specialized user group

Collection All materials (*q.v.*) comprising the intellectual content of the library

Library Includes all related terms such as information center, instructional media center, learning laboratory, documentation or referral center

Materials All media, both print and nonprint, visual and audio, which comprise the intellectual content of the library and the equipment necessary for their use

Unit (of library) Division, department, or office within the organization

NOTE: Comparison among tasks performed by the different categories of personnel should be made on the basis of the entire cluster of tasks within a subsystem or module, not on a task-by-task basis across the page. Task 1-P-1 is not specifically supported by 1-T-1 or 1-C-1.

1 COLLECTION DEVELOPMENT SUBSYSTEM

P Professional

1 Analyzes user needs and interests to determine future directions of collection
  1.1 Plans, conducts, and evaluates surveys of user needs and interests
  1.2 Evaluates patterns of materials use
  1.3 Consults with representatives of major user groups

2 Coordinates selection of materials with needs and resources of other appropriate libraries and organizations

3 Compiles lists of specific materials needed

4 Identifies availability of materials
  4.1 Examines dealers' stocks and displays
  4.2 Obtains information from publishers' representatives
  4.3 Examines materials sent on approval
  4.4 Reads trade publications and reviews

5 Selects materials
  5.1 Consults a variety of sources for information regarding, and evaluation of, materials being considered
  5.2 Evaluates materials directly by reading, listening to, or viewing
  5.3 Determines extent of duplication

T Technical

1 Searches for bibliographic information
  1.1 Checks standard tools for author information, publication data, and price
  1.2 Searches catalog and order files to determine if materials requested, or received under examination plan, are already in collection or on order
  1.3 Checks standard collection-building tools against catalog and notes materials not in collection
  1.4 Checks list of damaged and worn-out materials against standard tools to determine if they are still available for purchase

2 Assembles data for preparation of orders, including name of dealer, fund to which purchase is to be charged, number of copies and their distribution

3 Checks completed order forms for accuracy

4 Completes form letter or composes letter to dealer describing nature of incomplete or incorrect order and indicating action desired by library

5 Controls record of all serials acquired by library

C Clerical

1 Prepares orders for materials
  1.1 Types order forms from copy provided
  1.2 Sends to accounting unit order forms for materials requiring prepayment
  1.3 Types form letters and envelopes to accompany order forms
  1.4 Inserts order forms in envelopes for mailing
  1.5 Refers to supervisor orders involving vague and incomplete information, unusual costs, or departure from routine procedure
  1.6 Sends to cataloging and appropriate user-service units copies of completed order forms

2 Keeps records of orders
  2.1 Files order slips and forms
  2.2 Retrieves appropriate order forms from files when invoices arrive
  2.3 Routes approved invoices to accounting unit for payment
  2.4 Checks outstanding order files at regular intervals for items overdue

3 Checks materials received
  3.1 Opens and sorts materials received
  3.2 Checks materials received for damage

4 Verifies materials received
  4.1 Checks materials received against original orders for exact

P Professional (cont.)

desirable of specific materials

5.4 Decides among various editions of materials

5.5 Evaluates and makes decision on user requests for materials

5.6 Evaluates and makes decision on acceptability of gift materials

5.7 Decides among purchase, loan, reproduction, rental, or lease of materials

6 Makes decision on the withdrawal of materials from the collection

7 Procures through purchase, exchange, lease, rent, or gift, the materials selected

7.1 Ascertains availability of materials and prices

7.2 Maintains want lists for out-of-print titles and rare materials and bids on when they become available

7.3 Appraises specialized and rare materials

7.4 Negotiates contracts for prices and services with publishers, dealers, and jobbers

7.41 Selects jobber, dealer, or publisher to receive orders

7.5 Solicits gifts of materials library wishes to acquire

7.6 Establishes and supervises exchanges of materials with other libraries and organizations

8 Controls all stages of the acquisition process, including the rate of expenditure and the receipt of materials ordered

8.1 Establishes systems and procedures for purchase, exchange, lease, rent, or gift of materials

8.2 Establishes systems and procedures for recording

T Technical (cont.)

5.1 Produces at intervals, manually or by computer, lists of serials acquired by library

5.2 Answers questions and adjusts complaints from library units regarding lateness of delivery or nondelivery of serials

5.3 Sends to library units lists of serials for which subscriptions are about to expire and solicits recommendations for renewal or termination

5.4 Examines requests for serial back issues and replacements and orders materials following specific guidelines

6 Tests audio and video equipment

6.1 Tests equipment under consideration for acquisition and makes recommendations to professional staff

6.2 Examines and test-operates new equipment to insure proper functioning

7 Maintains accounting system for purchase of library materials

7.1 Operates accounting machine

7.2 Assigns budget account numbers for all new orders

7.3 Maintains list of materials purchased by price and account number

7.4 Prepares monthly and annual budget summary, showing by account number expenditures and balance

7.5 Maintains accounts by dealer or jobber

C Clerical (cont.)

titles, editions, number of copies, price

4.2 Checks materials received against invoices

4.3 Stamps and initials invoices to indicate correctness

4.4 Identifies incomplete or incorrect orders

5 Checks accuracy of invoices

5.1 Checks invoices for mathematical errors

5.2 Computes discounts

5.3 Converts foreign currency values to U.S. dollars

5.4 Compares dealers' statements claiming nonreceipt of payment against library records

6 Computes rental rates for rental materials and equipment

7 Compiles record, manually or by computer, of materials added to collection

7.1 Maintains file or inputs data, by author and title, and including date of acquisition, cost, and source, for materials added to collection

8 Compiles record, manually or by computer, of all serials acquired by library

8.1 Logs in master control file or inputs to computer, date and number of all serials received

8.2 Maintains record of missing issues

8.3 Completes form letter claiming undelivered issues

8.4 Maintains payment card for all subscriptions

P Professional (cont.)

    acquisition of materials, including all issues of serials

8.3 Controls budget for acquisition of materials

8.4 Schedules purchases, rentals, leases

8.5 Supervises the entire acquisition process and resolves difficult problems encountered

8.6 Determines unit or individual within library to examine materials received for consideration

8.7 Authorizes all orders

C Clerical (cont.)

8.5 Notifies supervisor when subscriptions do not arrive on time

8.6 Maintains history card for serials

8.7 Reviews file to determine if serials are on order

9 Performs other clerical tasks related to the acquisition of materials

9.1 Acknowledges gifts and exchanges

9.2 Records gifts and exchanges

9.3 Maintains address files of publishers, jobbers, and other suppliers of material

9.4 Returns to dealers, with form letter, materials sent on approval which are not being purchased or which have been sent in error

2 COLLECTION ORGANIZATION SUBSYSTEM

P Professional

1 Develops and expands classification systems

2 Establishes, and directs maintenance of, cataloging records

3 Supervises contributions to union catalogs and bibliographic centers and participates in cooperative cataloging arrangements

T Technical

1 Performs descriptive cataloging of materials for which LC cards or MARC tapes are not available

2 Catalogs fiction

3 Performs simple classification of materials identified in standard tools

C Clerical

1 Types cards or inputs data for catalogs, shelf list, and other files from copy provided

2 Reproduces cards in quantity by a variety of processes: tape, photocopy, multigraph, mimeograph

3 Arranges catalog cards in sets, following established procedures

P Professional (cont.)

4 Determines when reclassification or recataloging is needed and plans and supervises its performance

5 Assigns priorities to new materials to be processed

6 Assigns classification notation using Dewey, Library of Congress, Bliss, or other system, or local expansion or adaptation of one of these schemes

7 Assigns subject headings using standard tools and the library's own authority file

8 Adapts subject heading list to accommodate social and scientific changes, changes in reader interests, and use of new terminology

9 Reviews Library of Congress cards or MARC tapes and uses or adapts to local scheme

10 Determines number and kind of added entry cards required for new materials

11 Revises descriptive and fiction cataloging performed by technical staff

12 Designs filing systems for user services

T Technical (cont.)

4 Establishes form of author's name

5 Prepares for typist or data input operator copy for subject, author, and other cards
5.1 Checks cards for accuracy

6 Processes added copies and new editions
6.1 Has additional cards made if needed

7 Removes from catalogs and shelf list, manually or by computer, all records of materials which have been lost or withdrawn from the collection

8 Changes all appropriate records when materials are transferred from one unit of the library to another

9 Notes changes in titles of serials and inputs appropriate changes in catalog and other records

10 Revises filing of catalog cards performed by clerical staff

11 Supervises the physical upkeep of catalogs: shifting of cards, inserting of new guides, retyping of soiled and worn cards and guides

C Clerical (cont.)

4 Alphabetizes catalog cards, sets of cards, LC proof slips

5 Arranges shelf-list cards in class order

6 Does preliminary filing of cards in catalog

7 Files cards in shelf list and other files

8 Retypes cards, guides, and drawer labels

9 Inputs any changes in catalog and shelf list resulting from reclassification or recataloging

10 Separates by type computer-processed catalog cards

11 Orders cards from Library of Congress or other centralized service

12 Checks LC cards received against materials awaiting processing

13 Assigns book numbers
13.1 Checks Cutter-Sanborn tables for appropriate number
13.2 Consults shelf list to determine if other books have same number
13.3 Writes call number on title page

14 Adds date code to new materials

3 COLLECTION PREPARATION AND MAINTENANCE SUBSYSTEM

P Professional

1 Determines methods and techniques for the physical preparation, maintenance, and preservation of materials

2 Negotiates contracts with binding agents

3 Approves binding specifications

4 Makes final decision on whether deteriorating items are to be restored or microfilmed

5 Arranges for disposition of materials withdrawn from the collection by gift or exchange to other library, sale, or discard

T Technical

1 Inspects newly processed materials to make certain necessary pockets, cards, identifying labels have been properly completed

2 Maintains bindery control file

3 Sends materials to bindery with complete instructions as to fabric, color, and identification

4 Checks materials returned from bindery against original order with respect to both specifications and costs

5 Identifies titles unsuitable for binding and not in print and schedules for microfilming

6 Notes gaps in serial collections and recommends microfilming or purchase of back issues

C Clerical

1 Adds marks of ownership to new materials
  1.1 Stamps materials
  1.2 Hand-letters identification symbols

2 Color codes materials according to special characteristics

3 Places call numbers on materials by hand or machine or affixes labels

4 Prepares and affixes plates, pockets, cards, and labels to new or rebound materials
  4.1 Types information from copy provided
  4.2 Affixes labels or pockets by glueing
    4.21 Operates glueing machine
    4.22 Cleans and maintains glueing machine
  4.3 Shellacs over labels
  4.4 Inserts cards in pockets

5 Processes clippings
  5.1 Clips marked newspaper and magazine articles
  5.2 Stamps date and title of source publication on articles clipped
  5.3 Prepares clippings for filing by glueing or stapling on blank pages

6 Processes new filmstrips and tapes by attaching trailers and leaders

C Clerical (cont.)

7 Reviews shelves and files and
    removes materials in deteriorated
    condition

8 Sorts worn materials into: those that
    can be mended, those that require
    rebinding or major repair, and
    those that must be discarded

9 Examines for damage materials
    returned from circulation
   9.1 Rewinds and inspects film
   9.2 Removes phonograph records
       from jackets and inspects for
       breaks or scratches
   9.3 Plays tapes to inspect for
       erasures

10 Cleans materials and treats for
    preservation
   10.1 Cleans phonograph records
        returned from circulation
   10.2 Operates film-cleaning
        machine

11 Repairs worn or damaged materials
   11.1 Performs simple mending
        operations: taping, glueing
   11.2 Duplicates and inserts missing
        pages
   11.3 Splices tapes and filmstrips,
        using splicing machine or
        scissors and transparent tape

12 Makes and applies protective covers
    for materials
   12.1 Sorts materials by type of
        covering required
   12.2 Inserts periodicals, journals,
        reports, monographs in plastic
        covers, by hand or with
        binding machine

C Clerical (cont.)

12.3 Inserts pamphlets in binders or boxes
12.4 Reinforces pamphlets, booklets, and paperback books by taping spine and cover
12.5 Mends broken tape boxes, record albums, pamphlet boxes
12.6 Operates plastic laminator
12.7 Changes soiled plastic covers as required

13 Prepares purchase orders for titles to be sent to bindery

14 Sorts bound journals received from bindery by library units

4 COLLECTION STORAGE AND RETRIEVAL SUBSYSTEM

P Professional

1 Plans shelving arrangements and procedures

2 Plans shelf-reading and inventory operations

3 Coordinates space and time schedules for moving materials among units of library

T Technical

1 Supervises maintenance of shelves and files

2 Makes routine and spot inspections of shelves and files

3 Searches charge records, shelf lists, and other files to trace missing materials after routine check has been unsuccessful

4 Determines when materials are to be considered lost and notifies cataloging unit

C Clerical

1 Sorts returned materials by type, location, or unit of library to which assigned

2 Arranges returned materials numerically or alphabetically by information on spine or label

3 Moves materials to appropriate area by cart

4 Shelves materials by type, broad subject field, alphabetically, or

C Clerical (cont.)

numerically, by information on
spine or label

5 Files materials by indicated subject
headings or classification

6 Locates materials on shelves or in
files as requested, by information
provided on call slips or
announcement system

7 Delivers requested materials to
point of service in person or via
conveyor system

8 Searches shelves and files for
overdue materials

9 Makes regular examination of
shelves and files to determine if
materials are properly placed and
carded

10 Marks shelves and files, as
instructed, with subject headings
or classification numbers

11 Keeps shelves and files orderly by
proper alignment of materials
and use of supports and dividers

12 Clears tables in service areas,
returning materials to proper
places for reshelving or refiling

13 Shifts materials from one location to
another in accordance with
specific instructions

C Clerical (cont.)

14 Inventories shelves and files and
checks against circulation records
and shelf lists to determine if
materials are still in system

15 Places new materials on special
display shelves as instructed and
removes after specified time
interval to file or shelve in
permanent location

5 CIRCULATION SUBSYSTEM

P Professional

1 Establishes circulation system for all
types of materials

2 Receives and responds to sensitive
complaints and inquiries

3 Administers the library's interlibrary
loan policy
3.1 Coordinates policy with those
of neighboring libraries
3.2 Assists clerical and technical
staff with difficult bibliographic
searches
3.3 Exercises final approval on
loans

4 Supervises the establishment and
operation of reserve collections
of materials

T Technical

1 Supervises established circulation
and registration procedures

2 Responds to user complaints,
presented in person, by mail, or
telephone
2.1 Checks out reasons for problem
described
2.2 Interprets policies
2.3 Explains regulations
2.4 Corrects any errors in action or
procedure on the part of the
library
2.5 Refers to professional staff
problems on which assistance is
needed

3 Accounts for lost and damaged
materials
3.1 Checks charge records and
other files to trace missing
materials after routine checking
has been unsuccessful

C Clerical

a Registration Module

1 Explains the library's registration
policies and procedures
1.1 Gives applicants any printed
information available about the
library's services, collections,
and procedures

2 Checks to see if applicants have had
cards previously

3 Provides applicants with registration
forms and assists as required in
their completion

4 Reviews completed application
forms for completeness of
information
4.1 Obtains additional information
that may be required

T Technical (cont.)

3.2 Determines that materials under search are lost and conveys this information to appropriate units

3.3 Determines by established method amount to charge borrower for lost or damaged materials

4 Provides first-line supervision of interlibrary loan unit

4.1 Sorts mail, telephone, and TWX requests for loans and assigns to appropriate clerical staff

4.2 Provides clerical staff with needed instructions for processing

4.3 Approves loan orders for materials to leave unit

5 Provides first-line supervision of overdues process

5.1 Supervises process of notifying borrowers with overdue materials

5.2 Examines and verifies all fine charges or bills in excess of specified amount

5.3 Makes decision on reduction or cancellation of fines or bills when borrower questions in person, by telephone, or by letter

5.4 Seeks to obtain return of long-overdue materials by telephoning or going in person to home or office of borrower

5.5 Attempts to trace and locate borrowers with overdue materials who have left the jurisdiction of the library

5.6 Maintains list of borrowers whose library privileges have been cancelled for failure to return materials

C Clerical (cont.)

5 Determines whether to issue cards on the basis of information supplied

6 Types applicants' names and other identifying information on library cards

7 Issues cards to applicants

8 Maintains files of registrants

9 Records changes of address and retypes cards as requested by registrants

10 Withdraws expired cards from registration files

b Circulation Module

1 Charges, renews, and discharges circulating materials, using either manual or machine system

2 Instructs or assists borrowers as necessary in use of charging system

3 Checks to see if returned materials are overdue

4 Checks to see if returned materials are on reserve

5 Examines returned materials for obvious damage

C Clerical (cont.)

6 Answers borrowers' questions
concerning circulation rules

7 Where mail circulation service is
provided, sends materials to
shipping unit with appropriate
forms completed

8 Prepares circulation desk for service
8.1 Makes ready needed supplies
8.2 Changes dates in charging
system

9 Keeps circulation records
9.1 Files circulation cards by call
number
9.2 Keeps daily count of circulation
9.3 Compiles circulation statistics
at required intervals

c *Reserves Module*

1 Examines for completeness reserve
forms presented by users and
requests information not
provided

2 Checks to determine if material
requested on reserve order forms
is in circulation, on shelves, or
elsewhere in system

3 Locates cards for requested
materials already in circulation
and marks with identifying
symbol or attaches reserve order
forms

4 Identifies returned materials for
which reserve orders have been
placed and sets aside

C Clerical (cont.)

5 Inserts reserve slip in materials and files on shelves alphabetically by name of borrower who has placed reserve

6 Notifies borrowers by telephone or card of availability of material

7 Locates reserved materials upon presentation of notice by borrowers

d Overdues and Fines Module

1 Computes fines

2 Collects and records fines
   2.1 Operates cash register

3 Answers borrowers' questions regarding fines

4 Compiles, at required intervals, reports of fine income
   4.1 Operates adding machine

5 Verifies computer printouts of overdue materials

6 Completes and sends form notices to borrowers with overdue materials

7 Provides information to supervisor regarding borrowers who have not responded to form notices

C Clerical (cont.)

e Lost and Damaged Materials Module

1 Prepares form letter to go to
borrowers requesting payment
for lost or damaged materials

2 Records receipt of payment for lost
or damaged materials and
forwards money to accounting
unit

f Interlibrary Loan Module

1 Answers telephone and obtains
information necessary to process
requests

2 Separates and sorts received TWX
messages for interlibrary loan
materials and services

3 Types or writes order forms for
materials requested

4 Arranges all request forms in
sequential order (numerical or
alphabetical) before searching for
materials

5 Determines by checking catalogs
and circulation records if
requested materials are available

6 Searches shelves and files for
materials requested or completes
call slips for them

C Clerical (cont.)

7 Notifies borrower by form letter or TWX of availability of materials requested

8 Files requests by date of availability

9 Assigns borrower's number to all new requests

10 Computes postage and insurance rates (using standard tables) for materials being sent

11 Maintains files on all materials on interlibrary loan

12 Maintains record of dates on which materials are due to be returned

13 Requests return of overdue materials by telephone or card

14 Types cards with identifying information such as name of library, title, author, call number, borrower's name, and date due, for materials received from another library

15 Notifies borrowers by telephone or card when materials requested through interlibrary loan have arrived

16 Packages for return materials received through interlibrary loan

6 COLLECTION INTERPRETA-
TION AND USE SUBSYSTEM

P Professional

1 Provides assistance and guidance in the use of the collection to individuals and groups
  1.1 Explains the arrangement of the library
  1.2 Identifies types of materials available
  1.3 Answers questions regarding library's holdings
  1.4 Provides instruction, formal or informal, in use of bibliographic tools: catalogs, directories, indexes, files, and standard reference works

2 Provides reference assistance in person, by telephone, or by mail
  2.1 Locates the answers to informational questions
  2.2 Guides the user to sources of information
  2.3 Prepares special indexes
  2.4 Prepares specific reference reports
  2.5 Makes telephone calls for information not available in library's collection
  2.6 Abstracts materials

3 Provides guidance in users' selection of materials
  3.1 Provides information regarding specific materials and authors
  3.2 Informs users of materials relating to their special interests and needs
  3.3 Compiles selected lists of materials

T Technical

1 Performs simple bibliographic work under the supervision of professional staff
  1.1 Checks catalogs and standard sources for publication data needed for bibliographies
  1.2 Checks standard reference tools for information requested by professional staff

2 Assists users in the operation of video and audio equipment
  2.1 Schedules use of equipment
  2.2 Monitors use of equipment
  2.3 Provides instruction in operation
  2.4 Examines malfunctioning equipment in response to user requests
  2.5 Performs minor, on-the-scene maintenance

C Clerical

1 Makes photocopies of materials as requested by users

2 In response to user questions, provides directional information to major units of library

P Professional (cont.)

4 Evaluates users' reading, listening,
    and viewing skills and guides
    their development

5 Interprets and encourages the use of
    the library's resources
    5.1 Gives talks on general holdings
         and special collections and
         services
    5.2 Plans displays of library
         materials
    5.3 Selects materials for popular
         reading room
    5.4 Selects materials from new
         acquisitions for special display
    5.5 Supports and encourages
         library use through special
         programs and activities
    5.6 Conducts discussions of library
         materials
    5.7 Prepares discussion guides on
         library materials
    5.8 Recommends materials to
         individual users

6 Provides liaison with instructional
    programs
    6.1 Informs faculty and students of
         the personnel, materials, and
         equipment resources available
         in the library
    6.2 Advises faculty in utilizing the
         resources of the library in
         developing curriculum and
         course work
    6.3 Reviews and makes suggestions
         on materials lists provided by
         faculty
    6.4 Maintains liaison with faculty
         regarding reserve collection
         needs
    6.5 On request from faculty,
         arranges selections of materials
         on special topics
    6.6 Provides classroom collections
         of materials based on needs of

P Professional (cont.)

educational programs and
interests of students
6.7 Arranges for visits of classes to
library
6.8 Visits classrooms to introduce
materials of special interest,
give talks on library services,
and enroll students in special
library programs
6.9 Conducts workshops for faculty
in use of equipment available
in library

7 MANAGEMENT SUBSYSTEM

P Professional

a Planning Module

1 Formulates goals and objectives in
conjunction with colleagues and
the library's clientele

2 Formulates and recommends
policies and programs to
implement objectives

3 Interprets goals, objectives, and
policies
3.1 Formulates operating
procedures
3.2 Articulates policies and
procedures in written
statements and manuals

T Technical

a General Management Module

1 Serves as administrative secretary
1.1 Takes and transcribes minutes
of meetings
1.2 Prepares agendas
1.3 Makes arrangements for
meetings
1.4 Sends notices of meetings

2 Assembles data on library
operations, collection, and
services for use in reports, budget
requests, replies to inquiries, and
evaluative studies
2.1 Obtains data from appropriate
sources
2.2 Reduces statistical and
quantitative data to tabular or
graphic form

C Clerical

a Mail Module

1 Incoming mail:
1.1 Picks up at post office or
receiving unit
1.2 Sorts by unit or individual name
1.3 Opens items not specifically
addressed
1.31 Determines appropriate
unit to receive such items
1.4 Distributes to appropriate
individuals and units

2 Outgoing mail:
2.1 Folds and inserts letters in
envelopes by hand or machine
2.2 Packages materials
2.3 Weighs letters and packages
2.4 Computes postage and
insurance rates

P Professional (cont.)

4 Formulates and develops new
    service programs
   4.1 Articulates objectives to be
       served by them

5 Determines program priorities

6 Recommends allocation of financial,
    personnel, bibliographic,
    equipment, and space resources

7 Organizes the services and staffing
    of the library to meet its goals
    and objectives
   7.1 Designs, develops, and reviews
       organizational patterns within
       the library
   7.2 Determines level and nature of
       staffing required for
       organizational units

8 Conducts studies of library's
    systems and procedures and
    makes recommendations
    regarding them
   8.1 Recommends on basis of time,
       cost, and benefit factors,
       whether or not library processes
       be computerized
   8.2 Prepares flow charts and
       diagrams to define systems
       problems of library procedures

9 Evaluates policies and programs
   9.1 Establishes performance goals
      9.11 Monitors levels of goals
          achievement
   9.2 Establishes performance
       measures
      9.21 Determines nature of
          statistical data required

T Technical (cont.)

3 Organizes and supervises complex
    files
   3.1 Assigns subject headings

4 Serves as supervisor of major
    clerical unit

b Data Processing Module

1 Codes data for electronic processing

2 Writes computer programs
    following procedures outlined in
    flow charts

3 Performs desk checks of programs

4 Tests programs on computer

5 Checks data for accuracy upon
    completion of program execution

6 Corrects programs as necessary

7 Refines programs to reduce
    operating time

8 Classifies completed programs for
    storage and future use

9 Operates auxiliary electronic data
    processing equipment: sorters,
    collators, decollators, bursters,
    and slitters

C Clerical (cont.)

   2.5 Affixes postage by hand or
       machine
   2.6 Takes letters and packages to
       post office or central
       distribution unit

b Typing Module

1 Operates typewriter to produce
    letters, memoranda, cards,
    reports, lists, labels, and
    manuscripts
    From: handwritten or typed copy
      or dictation equipment
    In the form of: original and carbon
      copies, stencils, tapes, masters,
      and plates

2 Operates keypunch machine

3 Operates TWX machine

4 Operates computer input machine

5 Makes corrections of typed copy
    in a variety of forms

6 Maintains typewriter or other
    equipment in good working
    condition by performing simple
    cleaning and changing ribbons,
    tapes, and type faces

c Filing Module

1 Files correspondence, invoices,
    receipts, or other records by

T Technical (cont.)

10 Assists nontechnical staff in use of processed data

C Clerical (cont.)

alphabetical, numerical, subject, or other system

2 Organizes simple files
   2.1 Classifies materials

3 Prepares and affixes labels on folders and drawers

4 Retrieves materials from files as requested

5 Controls removal of materials from files and proper return thereof

6 Reviews files at regular intervals and removes older and less frequently needed materials

7 Maintains files in good condition, with folders, labels, and guides replaced as needed

d Stenographic Module

1 Takes dictation of letters, memoranda, and reports in shorthand or by machine, and transcribes, using typewriter

e Receptionist Module

1 Receives callers at library offices

2 Directs callers to appropriate individuals

3 Answers inquiries not requiring referral elsewhere

C Clerical (cont.)

f *Secretarial Module* [May also include some tasks listed under Mail, Typing, Filing, Stenographic, and Receptionist modules]

1 Schedules appointments for supervisor

2 Answers supervisor's telephone and refers calls, takes messages, or handles the business of the call

3 Acknowledges mail addressed to supervisor and responds to routine correspondence without dictation

g *Telephone Switchboard Module*

1 Operates telephone switchboard

2 Refers calls to proper units of library

3 Answers questions of a general nature such as hours of service

4 Places conference and long-distance calls

h *Reprography Module*

1 Determines best method of reproduction for the materials being copied

P Professional (cont.)	T Technical (cont.)	C Clerical (cont.)
		2 Operates multilith, mimeograph, addressograph, or photocopy machine
		3 Checks materials copied for acceptability and reproduces if necessary
		4 Services machines by replenishing paper, ink, toner, lubrication
		5 Cleans machines regularly
		6 Operates automatic paper punch, collator, paperfolding machine, and automatic stapling machine
		i Statistical Module
		1 Compiles, on instruction, statistics relating to library operations, collections, and services, for use in reports, budget requests, replies to inquiries, and evaluation studies
b Fiscal Module	*c Fiscal Module*	*j Fiscal Module*
1 Formulates the program needs of the library or organizational unit in terms of their estimated costs 1.1 Reviews and evaluates the proposals of component units 1.2 Integrates component requests into a unified proposal 1.3 Assembles data to support the needs expressed	1 Maintains library's accounting system 1.1 Sends verified accounts payable to heads of appropriate units for approval 1.2 Provides encumbrance reports to unit heads at stated intervals or on request 1.3 Prepares financial reports at stated intervals or on request	1 Writes checks for library, by hand or check-writing machine; maintains check register
		2 Prepares deposit slips
		3 Enters transactions in appropriate ledgers

P Professional (cont.)

2 Presents and interprets the budget proposal to appropriate decision-making levels
2.1 Reports on the progress of major programs and the library or unit's financial management

3 Administers the budget for the period established
3.1 Controls expenditures in conformity with the budget levels approved
3.2 Modifies programs as required by budgetary need
3.3 Establishes fiscal reporting system, including accounting procedures to be followed, expenditure periods to be used, and forms to be used

4 Analyzes sources of revenue, anticipates expenditures and costs of increased services

c Personnel Module

1 Plans and conducts programs of recruitment
1.1 Visits and conducts interviews in high schools, colleges, and graduate schools
1.2 Writes and places notices or advertisements of positions available in professional journals and local newspapers
1.3 Writes recruitment materials
1.4 Maintains liaison with academic and commercial placement agencies regarding the library's personnel needs
1.5 Posts vacancies at library conferences

T Technical (cont.)

1.4 Provides information to unit heads re accounting system or status of accounts
1.5 Provides information, as requested, to auditors

2 Handles banking activities of library, with responsibility for accuracy of accounts
2.1 Deposits all income for library in appropriate accounts
2.2 Controls access to, and use of, check-writing machine
2.3 Reconciles library accounts

3 Controls expense and cash funds in library
3.1 Controls use of petty cash fund
3.2 Reviews and pays authorized travel and expense accounts of staff
3.3 Reviews and approves requests to purchase routine supplies and equipment under specified amount

d Personnel Module

1 Interviews applicants for nonprofessional positions

2 Checks by telephone, letter, or form, references submitted by applicants

3 Writes letters of response, as delegated, to applicants for positions in library

C Clerical (cont.)

4 Maintains chronological account of expenditures by budget categories

5 Compiles expenditure totals for specific periods of time by budget categories

6 Checks cash reports received from library units

7 Checks invoices for mathematical errors

8 Handles petty cash funds on day-to-day basis

9 Operates accounting machines

k Personnel Module

1 Conducts typing tests of clerical applicants

2 Scores preemployment examinations that can be graded by keys

3 Maintains personnel files on all employees and former employees

4 Maintains a record, by pay-period intervals, of expenditures for personnel

action in relation to the information is frequently involved.

Observes operation of machine as work progresses, and makes adjustments to conform to blueprints and specifications.

Classifies aircraft flight data and submits data to Dispatcher for approval and flight authorization.

Collects background information on persons who are applying for credit, employment, insurance, or adjustments.

Collects, clarifies, and records forest data such as rainfall, stream flow, and soil moisture to develop information tables.

Summarizes details of transactions in separate ledgers and transfers data to general ledger to maintain records of financial transactions of an establishment.

Collects and arranges flight arrival and departure times at specified points to construct flight schedule.

Interviews applicants for employment and processes application forms according to established procedures.

Reviews electric power rates for conformity to schedule and prepares records pertaining to operative costs, revenues, and volume consumed.

Investigates complaints from public concerning crimes and police emergencies, records complaints, and files them for future processing.

Catalogs library materials such as books, films, and periodicals, according to subject matter.

Classifies and files musical recordings, sheet music, original arrangements, and scores for individual instruments.

Maintains inventory of goods in a stockroom.

Sells footware, such as shoes, boots, overshoes, and slippers in a department store.

COMPUTING: Performing arithmetic operations and reporting on and/or carrying out a prescribed action in relation to them. Does not include counting.

Calculates cost of customers' laundry by pricing each item on customers' lists, using adding machine, calculating machine, or comptometer.

Calculates interest and principal payments on mortgage loans, using calculating machine.

Figures and quotes repair cost estimates for hosiery and gloves.

Quotes tool-rental rates, prepares rental form, issues tool, and collects fee upon return of rental tool.

Calculates the amount of fabric required to produce specified styles of garments in various sizes, using size charts.

Figures daily wages of miners from production record.

Totals payments and proves daily transactions in a car rental establishment.

Makes change for payment received for food bill, cashes checks, and issues receipts or tickets to customers.

Calculates freight or passenger charges payable to participating carriers, using rate table and calculating machine.

Determines telephone charge of customer, according to time consumed, type of call, and rate of mileage zone.

Calculates payable odds to winning bets in gambling establishment and exchanges paper currency for playing chips or coin money.

Determines cost to customer of water conditioner based on frequency of service and size of unit required.

COPYING: Transcribing, entering, or posting data.

Enters information on manifest, such as name of shipper, tonnage, and destination from bills of lading and shipper's declaration.

Records meter readings such as oil, steam, temperature, and pressure on company operating chart.

Records style, color, and stock number of yard goods on warehouse card.

Transcribes written data from production department to punchcards by means of keypunch machine.

Enters test scores of applicants on permanent office record form.

Transcribes addresses from mailing list to envelopes, cards, advertising literature, packages, and similar items.

Records quantity and length of hides from tag on bundle.

Types letters, reports, stencils, forms, or other straight copy material from corrected rough draft.

Transcribes telephone numbers onto message slips, and forwards them to delivering personnel.

Records color, quantity, material, and part number from work ticket onto production report.

Posts totals of checks and drafts to clearinghouse settlement sheets.

Types reports, bills, application forms, shipping tickets, and other matter from clerical records.

Transcribes musical scores onto stencils, co-litho plates, or manuscript paper for reproduction.

Records odometer reading and amount of gas and oil used during refueling in vehicle log book.

Types notes and records of measurements, angles, elevations, and other data procured by surveying party.

COMPARING: Judging the readily observable functional, structural, or compositional characteristics (whether similar to or divergent from obvious standards) of data, people, or things.

Sorts and inspects telephone charge tickets for such billing information as destination of telegraph message and accuracy of telephone number to which charges are made.

Sorts and stacks hats, according to color, size, and style specified.

Inspects invoice of incoming articles with actual numbers and weights of articles.

Grades dressed poultry, according to size and quality.

Sorts burned clay products, such as brick, roofing tile and sewer pipe, according to form, color, and service characteristics.

Selects seasoned logs, following specification on work ticket, and examines wood for moisture content, following specified percentages.

Inspects candy in containers or on conveyor to insure that it is formed, coated, cupped, wrapped, or packed according to plant standards.

Locates and inspects conditions of assigned area of forest with respect to fire regulations to insure compliance by travelers and campers.

Examines painted surfaces of automobile to detect scratches, blemishes, and thin spots.

Inspects proof copy of Braille transcriptions against original script to detect errors and marks proofs for correction of grammatical, typographical, or compositional errors.

Walks between rails on railroad tracks to detect damaged, worn, or broken rails, pulled spikes or bolts, broken fish plates, soft beds, or wash-outs.

Inspects loaded freight cars to ascertain that materials and goods, such as automobiles, lumber, or containers of explosives are securely braced and blocked according to loading specifications.

Verifies weights marked on boxes or other containers for purposes of billing or verifying bill of lading.

Inspects washed automobiles at end of automatic car wash line to insure completeness of wash job.

PEOPLE FUNCTIONS

People: Human beings; also animals dealt with on an individual basis as if they were human.

MENTORING: Dealing with individuals in terms of their total personality in order to advise, counsel, and/or guide them with regard to problems that may be resolved by legal, scientific, clinical, spiritual, and/or other professional principles.

Renders consultation to those in physical or emotional distress to enhance their spiritual comfort.

Counsels clients in legal matters.

Works out plans with parents, teachers, and children, for overcoming problems in children who have behavioral, personality, or scholastic difficulties.

Works with parolees to assist them in rehabilitation and contacts employers to promote job opportunities for them.

Provides treatment for individuals with mental and emotional disorders.

Provides individuals with vocational and educational planning services, based on professional appraisal of their interests, aptitudes, temperaments, and other personality factors.

Counsels students in educational and personal-social activities and administers student personnel programs.

Advises and assists individuals in the solution of their socio-economic problems.

Guides juvenile campers by maintaining discipline, leading groups, and instructing individuals.

NEGOTIATING: Exchanging ideas, information, and opinions with others to formulate policies and programs and/or arrive jointly at decisions, conclusions, or solutions.

Negotiates with property owners and public officials to secure purchase or lease of land and right-of-way for utility lines, pipe lines, and other construction projects.

Contacts landowners and representatives of oil-producing firms in an attempt to complete agreements such as leases, options, and royalty contracts covering oil exploration, drilling, and production activities in specified oil fields.

Arranges with officials of various organizations in each locality to rent premises for a circus, to arrange for distribution of publicity and promotional materials, and to hire musicians for the circus band.

Participates in talks to settle labor disputes. Confers with union members and prepares cases for presentation. Meets with employers to negotiate or arbitrate.

Confers with foreign shippers to agree upon reciprocal freight handling contract.

Contracts with hospitals and other institutional agencies for students to obtain clinical experience in a school of nursing.

Meets with representatives of entertainment attractions such as troupes, performers, or motion picture distributors to arrange terms of contract and fees to be paid for engagement in establishments such as nightclubs, theaters, or dance halls.

Contracts with farmers to raise or purchase fruit or vegetable crops.

INSTRUCTING: Teaching subject matter to others, or training others (including animals) through explanation, demonstration, and supervised practice; or making recommendations on the basis of technical disciplines.

Trains nursing staff in techniques of industrial nursing. Conducts classes in first aid and home nursing for employees.

Conducts classes in instrumental or vocal music for individuals or groups in public or private school.

Provides training for police recruits in police science investigative methods and techniques, government, law, community life, marksmanship, self defense, and care of firearms.

Trains wild animals such as lions, tigers, bears, and elephants to perform tricks for entertainment of audience at circus or other exhibitions.

Teaches one or more subjects in a college or university classroom.

Coaches groups at playgrounds and schools in fundamentals and rules of competitive sports. Demonstrates techniques of a game and drills players in fundamentals until they are familiar with all its phases.

Lectures, demonstrates, and uses audiovisual teaching aids to present subject matter to class.

Illustrates and explains normal and emergency driving techniques and mechanical operation of automobile, using blackboard diagrams and audiovisual aids. Observes individuals in actual driving of automobile, explaining and demonstrating operation of brakes, clutch, and gearshift or automatic transmission.

Advises farmers concerning agricultural problems. Lectures and prepares articles on subjects such as farm arrangement and soil conservation. Demonstrates practical procedures used in solving agricultural problems.

Lectures and demonstrates job fundamentals to stewardesses of a passenger airline.

SUPERVISING: Determining or interpreting work procedures for a group of workers, assigning specific duties to them, maintaining harmonious relations among them, and promoting efficiency.

NOTE: A variety of responsibilities is involved in this function. While any of the following activities may indicate this function, usually a combination of them will be present in jobs appropriately rated for supervision:

Determines or interprets work procedures.

Assigns duties to workers.

Trains workers.

Evaluates workers' performances against standards.

Maintains harmonious relations among workers.

Promotes efficiency among workers.

Assists workers in solving work problems.

Initiates and/or recommends personnel actions such as firing, hiring, promoting, transferring, and disciplining.

Enforces company regulations.

Maintains or directs maintenance of records related to production and personnel.

Assigns guard force personnel to station or patrols. Interprets security rules and supervises subordinates in carrying out rules. Reports irregularities and hazards to appropriate personnel. Selects and trains subordinates. Insures that safety standards are maintained.

Has responsibility for workers engaged in loading ships' cargoes. Studies bills of lading to determine sequence of loading operations, calculates number of hours and personnel required, and assigns tasks to workers. Oversees workers to insure cargo is loaded in proper sequence.

Issues oral and written orders to newspaper workers engaged in gathering, writing, and publishing one type of news such as sports, society, music, drama, etc.

Directs the activities of workers engaged in distributing material to other workers and keeping records of parts worked on and completed.

Inspects engines and other equipment and orders ship crewmen to repair or replace defective parts.

Directs workers who maintain propulsion engines; boiler; deck machinery; and electrical, refrigeration, and sanitary equipment; and orders ship crewmen to repair or replace defective parts.

Interviews, hires, and gives instructions to fishing vessel crewmen, and assigns crew to watches and quarters. Directs fishing operations, using knowledge of fishing grounds and workload capacities of vessel and crew.

Establishes work procedures for workers engaged in loading and unloading kiln to dry green hops. Examines hops on kiln floor to determine distribution for drying, and gives instructions to workers concerning depth hops may be piled in kiln bay; and kiln temperature and air volume to be maintained.

Directs workers engaged in maintaining grounds and turf on golf course. Determines work priority and assigns workers to tasks such as fertilizing, seeding, mowing, raking, and spraying. Observes employees' work and demonstrates more efficient work methods.

DIVERTING: Amusing others. (Usually accomplished through the medium of stage, screen, television, or radio.)

Portrays role in dramatic production to entertain audience.

Sings classical, opera, church, or folk music in musical programs. Performs classical, modern, or acrobatic dances alone, with partner, or in groups to entertain audience.

Includes hypnotic trance in subjects, occasionally using members of audience as subjects, and commands hypnotized subjects to perform specific tasks.

Speaks in such a manner that voice appears to come from source other than own vocal chords, such as from dummy or hand puppet.

Performs original and stock tricks of illusion and sleight-of-hand to mystify audience, using props such as cards and cigarettes. Frequently uses members of audience in act.

Pilots airplane to perform stunts and aerial acrobatics at fairs and carnivals.

Dons diving suit and helmet, and drops to floor of tank to feed fish on scheduled show periods. Circulates among fish and identifies species and describes their life history in commentary over sound system.

Drives racing car over track in competition with other drivers.

Performs difficult and spectacular feats such as leaping, tumbling, and balancing, alone or as a member of team.

Professes to judge patron's character by studying his handwriting, observing details of letter formation.

Turns crank on portable barrel organ to play tunes. Trains and provides for monkey which accompanies him.

Impersonates Santa Claus during Christmas season.

PERSUADING: Influencing others in favor of a product, service, or point of view.

Confers with producers of crude oil and natural gas to purchase products at a favorable price.

Writes scripts for radio and television advertising.

Sells services of industrial psychology firms to management officials.

Calls on farmers to solicit repair business and to sell new milking equipment. Demonstrates milking machines.

Offers articles at auction, asking for bids, attempting to stimulate buying desire of bidders and closing sales to highest bidder.

Sells all types of life insurance by pointing out company programs that meet clients' insurance needs.

Plans or assists in advertising program to promote sale of company's product. Prepares advertising brochures and manuals for publication.

Writes comments on topics of current interest to stimulate or mold public opinion in accordance with viewpoints and policies of publication.

Solicits freight or storage business by visiting homes or business establishments to estimate cost of packing, crating, moving, shipping, and delivering household goods, machinery, or other material.

Contacts individuals and firms by telephone, in person, or by other means to solicit funds for charitable organization.

Sells home appliances to customer after pointing out salable features of merchandise.

Calls on retail outlets to suggest merchandising advantages of company's trading stamp plan.

Promotes use of and sells ethical drugs and other pharmaceutical products to doctors, dentists, hospitals, and retail and wholesale drug establishments.

SPEAKING-SIGNALING: Talking with and/or signaling people to convey or exchange information. Includes giving assignments and/or directions to helpers or assistants.

Directs traffic by motioning with flag when construction work obstructs normal traffic route.

Gives property man verbal directions in the placing of items on stage or set.

Confers with photographic staff to suggest improvements in artistry of camera shots.

Informs public on library activities, facilities, rules, and services.

Indicates customer bid by word, mannerism, hand, or other characteristic signal.

Interviews job applicants in an employment agency.

Answers questions from passengers concerning train routes, station, and timetable information.

Informs tourists concerning size, value, and history of establishment, points out features of interest, and gives other information peculiar to establishment.

Answers telephone to give information about company's special services to potential customers.

Signals or relays signals to operators of hoisting equipment engaged in raising or lowering loads and pumping or conveying materials.

Receives verbal complaints concerning mail delivery, mail theft, and lost mail.

Explains hunting and fishing laws to sportsmen.

Greets and introduces guests and suggests planned activities such as dancing or games.

SERVING: Attending to the needs or requests of people or animals or the expressed or implicit wishes of people. Immediate response is involved.

Receives payment for merchandise such as bakery goods, magazines, groceries, books, and tobacco selected by customer. Wraps or bags merchandise, and keeps shelves stocked with merchandise.

Rents bicycles to patrons at beach, resort, or similar recreational facility. Issues bicycle to customer, records time of transaction, and accepts payment.

Accompanies and assists ambulance driver on calls. Assists in lifting patient onto wheeled cart or stretcher and into and out of ambulance. Renders first aid such as bandaging, splinting, and administering oxygen.

Renders variety of personal services conducive to safety and comfort of airline passengers during flight.

Carries golf bags around golf course for players, handing clubs to players as requested.

Cares for elderly, handicapped, or convalescent people. Acts as aid or friend by attending to employer's personal, business or social needs.

Walks, rides bicycle, or uses public conveyances to make deliveries, and collects money from customers for cash-on-delivery orders.

Stands at upper or lower end of escalator to insure that passengers do not enter wrong conveyor. Assists elderly, infirm, or hesitant passengers in entering or leaving escalator.

Arranges wearing apparel and checks personal effects for performers and other personnel when they are on set.

Feeds and waters animals in a zoo, and cleans and disinfects their pens.

Mixes and serves alcoholic and non-alcoholic drinks following standard recipes to patrons of bar.

Bathes and gives alcohol rubs to hospital patients.

TAKING INSTRUCTIONS-HELPING: Attending to the work assignment instructions or orders of supervisor. (No immediate response required unless clarification of instructions or orders is needed.) Helping applies to "non-learning" helpers.

> *NOTE:* Taking Instructions-Helping, the lowest level worker function involving people, consists of receiving orders or instructions and/or helping others. Although this function is present to some degree in any functional responsibility involving people, it is possible to identify jobs where the functional involvement with people is at this prescribed level. No variety of responsibility is involved in this function, and any of the following situations will be rated for Taking Instructions-Helping:
> Receives instructions.
> Is informed of assignments, orders, etc.
> Helps and assists other workers.
> Obtains directions.

THINGS FUNCTIONS

Things: Inanimate objects as distinguished from human beings; substances or materials, machines, tools, equipment, and products. A thing is tangible and has shape, form, and other physical characteristics.

SETTING UP: Adjusting machines or equipment by replacing or altering tools, jigs, fixtures, and attachments to prepare them to perform their functions, change their performance, or restore their proper functioning if they break down. Workers who set up one or a number of machines for other workers or who set up and personally operate a variety of machines are included here.

Mounts reels of magnetic or paper tape onto spindles, decks of cards in hoppers, bank checks in magnetic ink readersorter, notices in optical scanner, or output forms and carriage tape in printing devices, to prepare off-line computer peripheral machines for operation. Sets guides, keys, and switches according to oral instructions or run book to prepare equipment to transfer data from one form to another, print output, and read data into and out of digital computer.

Unlocks ticket dispensing machines with key and turns knobs to reset number registers to zero. Changes code slugs so that different symbols are printed on tickets. Replaces depleted reels of ticket tape, threading ends of tape through feed rollers to type rollers. Presses keys of machines to obtain sample tickets. Examines tickets to ascertain that machines are printing correctly.

Selects, positions, and secures cutters in tool-head, in spindle, or on arbor of gear cutting machines such as gear shapers, hobbers, and generators. Sets feed rates and rotation speeds of cutters and workpiece in relation to each other by selecting and mounting gears, cams, or templates, or by moving levers. Moves controls to set cutting speeds and depth of stroke and cut for reciprocating cutters, and to position tools and workpieces.

Turns screws to adjust pockets of gathering machines to accommodate signatures. Turns dials to required graduation to set grippers and feelers according to thickness being gathered, using measuring instruments. Installs specified jogging trays at discharge end of machines and adjusts flow of glue and conveyor speed, using handtools. Starts machines to process sample copies and verify accuracy of machine setup before production run by machine operators.

Selects and positions, alines, and secures electrodes, jigs, holding fixtures, guides, and stops on resistance welding and brazing machines.

Lifts specified die sections into die-casting machines that cast parts such as automobile trim, carburetor housing, and motor parts from nonferrous metals. Secures die sections in position and adjusts stroke of rams. Connects water hoses to cooling system of die. Preheats die sections. Turns valves and sets dials to regulate flow of water circulating through dies. Starts machine to produce sample casting and examines casting to verify setup.

Selects, installs, and adjusts saw blades, cutter heads, boring bits, and sanding belts in a variety of woodworking machines, using handtools and rules. Operates machines to saw, smooth, shape, bore, and sand lumber and wood parts. Periodically verifies dimensions of parts for adherence to specifications, using gages and templates.

Determines tooling required according to specifications and knowledge of operations to be performed by multiple-spindle lathe-type machines equipped with automatic indexing and feeding mechanisms to perform turning, boring, threading, and facing operations. Installs collets, bushings, and stock pushers in stock-feeding mechanisms, using wrenches and screwdrivers. Installs and adjusts cams, gears, and stops. Starts machines and observes each operation. Verifies conformance of workpiece to specifications.

PRECISION WORKING: Using body members and/or tools or work aids to work, move, guide, or place objects or materials in situations where ultimate responsibility for the attainment of standards occurs and selection of appropriate tools, objects, or materials, and the adjustment of the tool to the task require exercise of considerable judgment.

Lays out position of parts on metal, using scribe and handtools.

Locates and marks reference lines such as centerlines, buttock lines, and frame lines and marks location of holes to be drilled, using scribe.

Uses water colors, brushes, pen, and rulers to sketch original designs for textile cloth patterns on graph paper.

Carves statues, monuments, and ornaments from stone, concrete, and wood, using chisels, hammers, and knives.

Polishes screwheads to specified dimensions and finish by fitting screws in circular multihole steel block, using tweezers and suction device; grinding blocked heads on bench mounted grinding wheel to remove burs; and polishing heads on bench flatlap polisher.

Lays out, cuts, shapes, and finishes wood, plastics, plexiglass, and hardboard parts of displays, using handtools.

Prepares scale and full size drawings for use by building contractors and craftsmen.

Diagnoses electrical malfunctions, using test lights, ohmmeters, voltmeters, circuit simulators, and wiring diagrams.

Pulls bow across strings of violin with one hand and presses strings with fingers of other hand to produce desired effects.

Inspects machined parts and assembled units for conformance to specifications, using micrometers, gages, calipers, and other precision measuring instruments.

Cuts, trims, and tapers hair, using clippers, comb, and scissors.

Measures, marks, and cuts carpeting and linoleum with knife to get maximum number of usable pieces from standard size rolls, following floor dimensions and diagrams.

Forms sand molds for production of metal casting, using handtools, power tools, patterns, and flasks; and applying knowledge of variables such as metal characteristics, molding sand, contours of patterns, and pouring procedures.

Sketches design, using pencil or permanent ink. Grinds colors on pottery tile, using palette knife to mix colors and oils to desired consistency. Paints freehand or within sketched design, using mixed colors, or applies pure colors, one over another, to produce desired shade.

OPERATING-CONTROLLING: Starting, stopping, controlling, and adjusting the progress of a machine or equipment. Operating involves setting up and adjusting the machine or material(s) as the work progresses. Controlling involves observing gages, dials, etc. and turning valves and other devices to regulate factors such as temperature, pressure, flow of liquids, speed of pumps, and reactions of materials.

Turns controls on television camera; observes scenes through camera monitor; adjusts lens to maintain scenes in focus; and moves levers to alter angle or distance of shot to photograph scenes for broadcasting.

Places wooden barrel horizontally on barrel rest of barrel lathe machine. Clamps barrel between two chucks of the lathe. Starts machine and holds barrel plane against surface of revolving barrel while guiding tool along its length to scrape and smooth it.

Attaches skip bar to key punch machine. Loads machine with decks of punchcards. Moves switches and depresses keys to select duplication, spacing, and transfer of cards through machine station.

Moves lever to regulate speed of turntable of tape recorder machines. Turns knobs on cutting arms to shift or adjust weight of stylus. Moves switches to open microphone and tune in live or recorded programs.

Clamps sample of tinplate on scribing table and outlines specified areas to be coated, using scriber. Moves coater machine lever to raise uncoated tinplate into feeding position. Adjusts or changes gears of feeding mechanism to regulate rate of feed. Adjusts rollers to regulate thickness of coating materials on plate, using wrenches and rule.

Positions and bolts or clamps single or multiple dies on bed of printing press, using hand-tools. Loads coil of strip metal on machine spindle, feeds strip between dies, turns hand-wheels to close and tighten dies on metal strip and starts machine.

Places glass blanks and tube components in chuck or tailstock of lathes and depresses pedals of compressed air devices that lock parts in lathes. Starts lathes, lights gas-torch heating elements and turns valves to regulate flames. Turns handwheels or pushes levers to control heating of specified areas of glass parts.

Places spool on spindle of floor-mounted sewing machines. Draws thread through machine guides, tensions, and needle eye. Inserts bobbins into shuttles and draws thread through slots in shuttle walls or draws thread through guides and looper eyes. Presses knee levers, depresses pedals, or moves hand levers to raise presser foot or spread feed cups. Positions parts to be joined and lowers presser foot. Starts, stops, and controls speed of machines with pedals or knee levers and guides parts under needles.

Moves switches on central control panel of switchboard to regulate converters. Observes demand meters, gages, and recording instruments, and moves controls to insure efficient power utilization, equipment operation, and maintenance of power distribution. Monitors gages, alarms and oscilloscopes to detect and prevent damage to equipment and disruption of power.

Selects specified embossing plate, bolts plate into chase, and positions and secures chase onto ram of embossing machine used to imprint designs on leather or leather articles. Turns switch or steam valve to heat plate to specified temperature, according to type of leather. Pulls lever that lowers ram to impress designs on leather.

Fires furnace or kiln, observes gages, and adjusts controls to maintain specified temperature for drying coal and ore before or after washing, milling, or pelletizing operations.

Regulates flow and pressure of gas from mains to fuel feed lines of gas-fired boilers, furnaces, kilns, soaking pits, smelters, and related steam-generating or heating equipment. Opens valve on feed lines to supply adequate gas for fuel, and closes valves to reduce gas pressure. Observes, records, and reports flow and pressure gage readings on gas mains and fuel feed lines.

Types payroll.

DRIVING-OPERATING: Starting, stopping, and controlling the actions of machines or equipment for which a course must be steered, or which must be guided, in order to fabricate, process, and/or move things or people.

NOTE: Involves such activities as observing gages and dials; estimating distances and determining speed and direction of other objects; turning cranks and wheels; pushing or pulling gear lifts or levers. Includes such machines as cranes, conveyor systems, tractors, furnace charging machines, paving machines, and hoisting machines. Excludes manually powered machines, such as handtrucks and dollies, and power assisted machines, such as electric wheelbarrows and handtrucks.

Steers vessel over course indicated by electronic equipment, such as radio, fathometer, and land radar to transport passengers to fishing locations for catching fish and other marine life.

Pushes pedals and pulls levers to move, control speed and stop crane, turn crane boom, and raise or lower cables attached to load. Adjusts controls to move and position load by sight or at direction of other worker.

Pilots airplane or helicopter over agricultural fields at low altitudes to dust or spray fields with seeds, fertilizers, or pesticides.

Operates throttle, air brakes, and other controls to transport passengers or freight on electric, diesel-electric, steam, or gas-turbine-electric locomotive. Interprets train orders, block or semaphore signals, and railroad rules and regulations.

Fastens attachments, such as graders, plows, and rollers to tractor with hitchpins. Releases brake, shifts gears, and depresses accelerator or moves throttle to control forward and backward movement of machine. Steers tractor by turning steering wheel and depressing brake pedals.

Pushes levers and pedals to move machine, to lower and position dipper into material, and to lift, swing, and dump contents of dipper into truck, car, or onto conveyor or stock pile.

Moves control levers, cables, or other devices to control movement of elevator. Opens and closes safety gate and door of elevator at each floor where stop is made.

Controls movement and stops railroad or mine cars by switching, applying brakes, placing sprags (rods) between wheelspokes, or placing wooden wedges between wheel and rail. Positions cars under loading chutes by inserting pinch bar under car wheels, using bar as fulcrum and lever to move car. Hooks cable to car and controls cable drum brake to ease car down incline.

Moves controls to steer armored car to deliver money and valuables to business establishments.

Controls action of rail-mounted trackmobile to spot railroad cars on ramp above chip storage bins for unloading, and releases bottom doors of cars allowing chips to fall into bin.

Moves controls to activate rotary brushes and spray so that sweeping machine picks up dirt and trash from paved street and deposits it in the dirt trap in rear of machine.

MANIPULATING: Using body members, tools, or special devices to work, move, guide, or place objects or materials. Involves some latitude for judgment with regard to precision attained and selecting appropriate tool, object, or material, although this is readily manifest.

Shapes knitted garment after cleaning by shrinking or stretching garments by hand to conform to original measurements.

Trims and smooths edges, surfaces, and impressed or raised designs of jewelry articles and jewelry findings, using files, chisels, and saws.

Scrapes, files, and sands machine-shaped gunstocks to remove excess wood and impart finished appearance to surface, using files, sandpaper, and emery cloth.

Draws different color strips of material such as fabric of leather between slits in shoe upper to weave decorative design, according to specifications.

Turns sprayer valves and nozzle to regulate width and pressure of spray, pulls trigger and directs spray onto work surface to apply prime or finish coat, according to knowledge of painting techniques.

Guides tip of soldering iron along seam of metal plates to heat plates to bonding temperature and dips bar or wire of soft solder in seam to solder joint.

Mixes soldering flux in crock or vat, according to formula, using paddle, and tests consistency of flux with hydrometer.

Repacks parachutes that have been opened in use, or unopened ones that are to be repacked in interest of safety.

Attaches cables to buildings, installs supports, and cuts or drills holes in walls and partitions through which cables are extended, using wrenches, pliers, screwdrivers, saws, and drills.

TENDING: Starting, stopping, and observing the functioning of machines and equipment. Involves adjusting materials or controls of the machine, such as changing guides, adjusting timers and temperature gages, turning valves to allow flow of materials, and flipping switches in response to lights. Little judgment is involved in making these adjustments.

Positions and secures scoring disks on machine shaft, turns handwheel to adjust pressure on disks, and feeds cardboard blanks into machine hopper.

Turns controls to regulate amount of coal, pushes air blowers controls that blow coal into furnaces, and observes air gages and feed of coal.

Presses pedal or button, and moves lever on packaging machine. Observes operation to detect malfunctions. Opens valves, changes cutting dies, sets guides, and clears away damaged products or containers.

Lights fire and opens valves to regulate fuel supply to asphalt-heater. Screws hose connections to heater to connect circulating system, and uses pump to circulate asphalt through heating unit. Observes temperature gage and adjusts blower and damper controls to regulate heat and maintain required temperature.

Adjusts control that regulates stroke of paper pusher on machine that assembles pages of printed material in numerical sequence. Places pages to be assembled in holding tray. Turns controls manually to start machine and removes assembled pages from machine.

Depresses pedal to start, stop, and control speed of yarn winding machine. Observes yarn to detect slubs and broken or tangled ends, cuts out slubs, using scissors, and ties broken yarn ends.

Positions spring on bed of machine, turns hand gages to regulate travel of flattening ram, and pulls lever to lower ram that compresses spring under specified pressure.

Places tack in holder on machine bed. Positions premarked article over tack on bed and positions button on garment over tack and under machine ram. Depresses pedal that lowers ram to join button to article.

Shovels coal or coke into firebox of boiler, turns valves to regulate flow of gas, oil, or pulverized coal into firebox, or moves controls to regulate feeding speed of automatic stoker. Reads gages and moves controls to maintain specified steam pressure, temperature, and water level in boiler.

FEEDING-OFFBEARING: Inserting, throwing, dumping, or placing materials in or removing them from machines or equipment which are automatic or tended or operated by other workers.

Inserts milled rubber stock into rolls of calendaring machine to maintain continuous supply.

Places molded lens blanks into automatic bur-grinding machine. Catches ejected blanks and stacks them in trays prior to polishing.

Picks up and dumps specified dry materials into feeder hopper of crutcher equipment which forms slurry for processing into soap.

Hangs toy parts in specified positions on hooks of overhead conveyor that passes through painting operations and lifts painted parts from hooks.

Places eggs in holder that carries them into machine that removes earth, straw, and other residue from egg surface prior to shipment. Removes cleaned eggs and packs them in cases.

Places plate glass onto conveyor of glass silvering machine or automatic washing and drying machines, and removes silvered or cleaned mirror from conveyor.

Shovels scrap tobacco onto screens of cleaning machine, picks out stems and dirt from tobacco, and shovels tobacco dust from receptacle under screen into containers.

Dumps dyed cotton fiber into hopper of extractor that removes liquid by forcing cotton through rollers.

Places soiled garments into washing machine, extractor, and tumbler, and removes garments at completion of cleaning cycle.

Places uncured sponge rubber blanks in cavities of hard rubber molds, positions filled molds on conveyor of vulcanizing press, and unloads vulcanized arch cushions from machine.

HANDLING: Using body members, handtools, and/or special devices to work, move, or carry objects or materials. Involves little or no latitude for judgment with regard to attainment of standards or in selecting appropriate tool, object, or material.

Loads and pushes handtruck to move metal molds of pipemaking concrete from forming area to steam-cooking area.

Hammers steel pins into holes in ends of logs preparatory to skidding.

Drives flock of goats to fresh pastures during day and back to corral at night.

Clears stumps, trees, brush, cactus, mesquite, or other growth from land so land can be used as pasture, for cultivation, or for proposed construction project.

Weighs materials in chemical plant and writes or stencils identifying information on containers. Fastens caps or covers on containers, or screws bungs in place. Transports materials, using handtruck. Cleans stills and other equipment, using detergents. Loads railroad cars or trucks.

Distributes work cards containing instructions to workers.

Scrubs and washes surgical instruments.

Mops, sweeps, and dusts halls and corridors.

Digs ditches that drain excess moisture from land, using pick and shovel.

Loads handtruck with ingots or sorted scrap.

Lifts plastic forms used in molding process from self-sealing fuel tanks.

Wipes cured tires with soapstone powder to dry them.

Uses knife to cut candy into squares.

Folds and stacks cuffs preparatory to sewing cuffs to sleeves of garments.

Scrapes or knocks mortar from bricks, using hammer.

Handles sheet music when rehearsing for performance as soloist or as member of vocal ensemble.

Uses pen to write magazine articles.

WORK FIELDS

Alphabetical Listing of Work Fields

051	Abrading
291	Accommodating
232	Accounting-Recording
295	Administering
211	Appraising
141	Baking-Drying
005	Blasting
071	Bolting-Screwing
053	Boring
153	Brushing-Spraying
034	Butchering
094	Calking
132	Casting
052	Chipping
031	Cleaning
161	Combing-Napping
263	Composing
146	Cooking-Food Preparing
003	Cropping
142	Crushing
135	Die Sizing
202	Developing-Printing
144	Distilling
242	Drafting
111	Electrical Fabricating-Installing-Repairing
112	Electronic Fabricating-Installing-Repairing
122	Electro-Mechanical Fabricating-Installing-Repairing
154	Electroplating
244	Engineering
183	Engraving
297	Entertaining
181	Eroding
182	Etching
041	Filling
145	Filtering-Straining-Separating
061	Fitting-Placing
082	Flame Cutting-Arc Cutting
062	Folding-Fastening
006	Gardening
063	Gluing
294	Healing-Caring
133	Heat Conditioning
012	Hoisting-Conveying
001	Hunting-Fishing
151	Immersing-Coating
192	Imprinting
282	Information Giving
271	Investigating
032	Ironing
165	Knitting

092	Laying
241	Laying Out
272	Litigating
011	Loading-Moving
002	Logging
033	Lubricating
057	Machining
091	Masoning
121	Mechanical Fabricating-Installing-Repairing
131	Melting
292	Merchandising
055	Milling-Turning-Planing
004	Mining-Quarrying-Earth Boring
143	Mixing
136	Molding
072	Nailing
042	Packing
262	Painting
201	Photographing
134	Pressing-Forging
191	Printing
147	Processing-Compounding
293	Protecting
014	Pumping
231	Recording
251	Researching
073	Riveting
152	Saturating
056	Sawing
171	Sewing-Tailoring
054	Shearing-Shaving
083	Soldering
162	Spinning
021	Stationary Engineering
221	Stock Checking
101	Structural Fabricating-Installing-Repairing
264	Styling
243	Surveying
281	System Communicating
296	Teaching
013	Transporting
093	Troweling
298	Undertaking
102	Upholstering
164	Weaving
212	Weighing
081	Welding
163	Winding
043	Wrapping
261	Writing

Work Field Organization

The Work Fields, as listed below, have been organized into groups on the basis of similar technology, or overall socioeconomic objective.

ORGANIZATION	DESCRIPTION
001 Hunting-Fishing 002 Logging 003 Cropping 004 Mining-Quarrying-Earth Boring 005 Blasting 006 Gardening	Securing, producing, or cultivating raw materials, products, or animals (livestock or game) on or below the surface of the earth; usually outdoor work.
011 Loading-Moving 012 Hoisting-Conveying 013 Transporting 014 Pumping	Moving materials (in solid, liquid, or gaseous form) or people, by hand and/or machine power.
021 Stationary Engineering	Producing and/or distributing heat, power, or conditioned air.
031 Cleaning 032 Ironing 033 Lubricating 034 Butchering	Cleaning and maintenance work.
041 Filling 042 Packing 043 Wrapping	Packaging materials or products for distribution or storage.
051 Abrading 052 Chipping 053 Boring 054 Shearing-Shaving 055 Milling-Turning-Planing 056 Sawing 057 Machining	Working with machines and/or handtools to cut or shape wood, metal, plastics, or other materials, or objects made from these materials. Can also involve assembly of objects.
061 Fitting-Placing 062 Folding-Fastening 063 Gluing	Assembling materials, usually light.
071 Bolting-Screwing 072 Nailing 073 Riveting	Assembling part or materials, usually of metal, wood, or plastics, by means of screws, nails, or rivets.
081 Welding 082 Flame Cutting-Arc Cutting 083 Soldering	Bonding or cutting materials by means of a gas flame, electric arc, combination welding process, or soldering.
091 Masoning 092 Laying 093 Troweling 094 Calking	Working with brick, cement, mortar, stone, or other building materials (other than wood) to build or repair structures, or to assemble structural parts.

ORGANIZATION	DESCRIPTION
101 Upholstering	All-round fabricating, installing, and/
102 Structural Fabricating-Installing-Repairing	or repairing of interior fittings; structures; and electrical, electronic, and
111 Electrical Fabricating-Installing-Repairing	mechanical units. Involves combinations of other Work Fields, usually 051
112 Electronic Fabricating-Installing-Repairing	through 094.
121 Mechanical Fabricating-Installing-Repairing	
122 Electro-Mechanical Fabricating-Installing-Repairing	
131 Melting	Compounding, melting, heat conditioning,
132 Casting	and shaping metal and plastics, by
133 Heat Conditioning	any method in which heat is a factor.
134 Pressing-Forging	
135 Die Sizing	
136 Molding	
141 Baking-Drying	Processing various materials, in solid,
142 Crushing	fluid, semi-fluid, or gaseous states, during
143 Mixing	production process or to prepare
144 Distilling	for distribution.
145 Filtering-Straining-Separating	
146 Cooking-Food Preparing	
147 Processing-Compounding	
151 Immersing-Coating	Coating or impregnating materials and
152 Saturating	products to impart decorative or protective
153 Brushing-Spraying	finish or other specific quality,
154 Electroplating	as described under separate Work Field sections.
161 Combing-Napping	Processing fibers from thread to fabric.
162 Spinning	
163 Winding	
164 Weaving	
165 Knitting	
171 Sewing-Tailoring	Joining, mending, or fastening materials with needle and thread, and fitting and adjusting parts.
181 Eroding	Cutting designs or letters into materials
182 Etching	or products by sandblasting (Eroding),
183 Engraving	applying acids (Etching), or action of sharp pointed tools (Engraving).
191 Printing	Transferring letters or designs onto
192 Imprinting	paper or other material, by use of ink or pressure, includes setting type and preparing plates.
201 Photographing	Taking pictures and developing and
202 Developing-Printing	processing film.

ORGANIZATION	DESCRIPTION
211 Appraising 212 Weighing	Evaluating or estimating the quality, quantity, or value of things or data; ascertaining the weight of materials or objects.
221 Stock Checking	Receiving, storing, issuing, shipping, requisitioning, and accounting for stores of materials.
231 Recording 232 Accounting-Recording	Preparing and maintaining verbal and/or numerical records.
241 Laying Out 242 Drafting 243 Surveying 244 Engineering	Plotting, tracing, or drawing diagrams and other directive graphic information for use in design or production; designing and constructing machinery, structures, or systems.
251 Research	Controlled exploration of fundamental areas of knowledge, by means of critical and exhaustive investigation and experimentation.
261 Writing 262 Painting 263 Composing 264 Styling	Creative work.
271 Investigating 272 Litigating	Dealing with people to gather information to carry out business or legal procedures.
281 System Communicating 282 Information-Giving	Provides, or effects the transmission of, information to other persons, indirectly (by electrical or electronic media) or directly (by voice or written statement).
291 Accommodating 292 Merchandising 293 Protecting 294 Healing-Caring 295 Administering 296 Teaching 297 Entertaining 298 Undertaking	Dealing with people to provide services of various types.

BACKGROUND OF THE EVALUATION SYSTEM
for
ADMINISTRATIVE, PROFESSIONAL, AND TECHNOLOGICAL POSITIONS

For evaluation purposes, the Task Force has grouped Federal positions into six broad categories. Models for evaluating positions in these categories are in various stages of development and testing. The Administrative, Professional, and Technological category covers most nonsupervisory positions in the Federal Government that possess similar characteristics to those nonsupervisory jobs classified as exempt* status employees in private industry. Other models under development are: Executive Evaluation System (EES), which will be available for agencies to use in ranking positions in the Federal Executive Service; Clerical, Office Machine Operation, and Technician Evaluation System (COMOT) applicable to production-oriented jobs requiring nonprofessional qualifications; Special Occupations Evaluation Systems (SOES), designed for ranking positions and personal competence of incumbents in occupations such as teachers, attorneys, doctors and nurses, scientists and engineers engaged in research and development work, and certain protective jobs; and Supervisor and Manager Evaluation System (SAMES), which is to be used in evaluating all such jobs regardless of occupation. It is anticipated that the Coordinated Federal Wage System (CFWS) will remain essentially unchanged except for the transfer of certain supervisory positions to SAMES.

In some instances, other evaluation systems will be closely linked with APTES. The need for linkage between APTES and SAMES and EES is apparent and will be dealt with in the design of those systems. SOES present a somewhat unique problem of relationships since those systems introduce level of personal competency into the ranking process. Benchmark job descriptions for one or more key tie-in levels in several of these occupations have been included in the APTES model, i.e., nurse, physician, research scientist. However, incumbents would actually be ranked under the appropriate system. The SOES may be viewed as extensions to APTES. Since each of the SOES is unique, the linkage with APTES will be included in their design.

The Administrative, Professional, and Technological Evaluation System (hereafter abbreviated APTES) covers approximately 600,000 nonsupervisory positions currently allocated to one of 75 administrative, 137 professional, and 98 technological class series in the General Schedule. More specifically, the occupations covered in the three broad subgroupings are:

a. Administrative. This group includes occupations where entrants frequently have college-level education, but there normally is no qualification requirement for specialized subject-matter courses. Included are such occupations as personnel, procurement, budgeting, management analysis, etc.

b. Professional. This group includes occupations where typically there is a positive educational requirement for entrance, normally obtained by a baccalaureate or higher degree in a university or equivalent institution of higher learning, with a major in the area of the profession. This includes physical and social science professions, mathematics, law, health professions, engineering, accounting, and education.

c. Technological. This group includes occupations where entrants frequently have specialized technical education or the necessary specialized training and experience acquired on the job. These positions are often closely associated with occupations in the professional or administrative groupings, and for the occupations under the General Schedule currently have a similar grade pattern. Included are computer specialist positions, most inspector jobs, and various specialized technical, regulatory and enforcement occupations such as tax auditors.

---

* That is, exempt as defined under the provisions of the Fair Labor Standards Act of 1938.

This material was developed by the Job Evaluation and Pay Review Task Force, U.S. Civil Service Commission.

Need for a New Approach

The Task Force's investigations revealed a number of inadequacies in the position classification system as applied to this group of positions which, in its opinion, cannot be adequately
corrected by simply modifying the present system. Some of these problems are:

--The current occupational grade alignment within this category does not permit
   reasonable comparability with private industry in setting pay rates for many of
   the occupations.

--There are more grade levels used in the General Schedule for some individual
   occupations than there are clearly identifiable levels of work.

--The present classification standards have weaknesses; i.e., some standards are
   written in terms too general to be specifically applicable, some do not define the
   full range of either levels or kinds of work in a given series adequately, and some
   standards appear to define artificial levels.

The conclusions of the Task Force thus confirm the findings of the House Subcommittee
Position Classification Report that the present General Schedule system is too complex and
requires more time and effort than is available to adequately maintain it.

Practices of Other Employers Explored

With the deficiencies of the present system in mind, the Task Force investigated various
systems now in use in the Federal Government--i.e., Atomic Energy Commission, National
Security Agency, etc.--and those used by the more progressive State governments and major
private employers to determine what methodology of job evaluation would best fit the current
needs of the Federal service. The factor ranking method with benchmark job descriptions and
guide charts was found to utilize techniques which overcome the deficiencies of the present
classification system. Factor ranking is essentially a technique of comparing the job to be
evaluated with all others, one factor at a time. The technique forces the rater to make
critical analyses of the job on a factor basis, each job in relation to each other. A
system of benchmark job descriptions extends the adaptability of the evaluation system to a
wide variety of jobs and work situations and gives the user clear-cut standards and guidelines for application of the guide charts. In varying forms, this method has been widely
used successfully in private industry and the basic methodology is well established.

Basic Concept of the System

The factor ranking system as conceived for possible application to the administrative,
professional, and technological category jobs consists of:

--Definition of factors to be used in measuring the relative worth of jobs.

--A system of benchmark jobs described in terms of the significant factors and
   representative of the full range of jobs to be covered by the system. (Initially
   a limited sample of generally Government-wide benchmarks have been defined.) It
   is contemplated that additional benchmark jobs will be later prepared by the
   Civil Service Commission and agencies to cover key jobs throughout the agency and
   Government job population.

--Factor rating scales which identify the measurable levels within each factor and
   provide appropriate numerical values for each level.

--A simple set of instructions, reference keys, and conversion tables.

The benchmark positions serve as the key element in this system. They are the standards and
guides for the evaluation of positions and for interpretation and application of the factor

rating scales. As the system becomes fully implemented each user will have a set of
relevant and familar approved benchmark descriptions to guide his decisions in evaluating
positions. The factor rating scales give the user an overall view of the system and the
interrelationship among the several factors. The scales are also used in making inter-
occupational comparisons. The rating scales are particularly helpful in evaluating new jobs
for which job relationship patterns have not yet been established. New benchmark position
descriptions can be added to the system with relative ease. This will permit the system to
be quickly responsive to the dynamics of a changing Federal work force. This type of system
can be used to evaluate a wide variety of jobs with reasonable assurance of consistency of
job treatment among agencies. Thus, the system has potentially many positive advantages
over the present position classification system. In addition, the total system consisting
of factor rating scales backed up by very specific benchmark positions can reduce
significantly the opportunities for abuse.

Concept of Administration of the System

It is envisioned that the Civil Service Commission will maintain control over the benchmark
positions used on a Government-wide basis. Individual agencies would prepare and use
additional benchmark positions subject to approval by the Civil Service Commission. Field
installations and subordinate units of an agency would also prepare benchmark descriptions
for their unique positions, subject to approval by their next higher agency echelon. As is
true under the current General Schedule system, agencies would have responsibility for
assigning individual positions to appropriate skill levels. However, preliminary studies
indicate that the technique is one that is relatively easy for line managers and employees
to use and understand. Therefore, the system will permit agencies to delegate position
evaluation authority to managers well down in an agency's organization.

Basic Procedures Followed in Developing the System

Selecting and Defining Factors

The significant factors and subelements to be used in measuring the relative worth of work
were identified through a review of the nature of the work included in occupations in the
APTES category. A survey was also made of the factors used in other evaluation systems for
similar occupations. The considerations in selection of factors were that they are:

--Measures of significant and distinct characteristics of work.

--Applicable to all positions but in varying degrees.

--Ratable in terms of recognizable and definable differences in level.

--Have a minimum of overlap between them.

Five factors were selected and these are:

Factor I. Job Requirements
This factor measures the nature and extent and level of knowledge
and abilities needed to perform work acceptably.

Factor II. Difficulty of Work
This factor measures the complexity or intricacy of work and mental
demands, i.e., judgment, originality, and other mental effort required,
as affected by quality and relevance of the available guidelines.

Factor III. Responsibility
This factor measures the assistance and control provided by the supervisor and the impact of work on the accomplishment of the mission of the
organization.

Factor   IV.   Personal Relationships
This factor measures the skill required in work relationships with others and the importance of such relationships to the success of the work.

Factor   V.   Other Requirements
This factor measures any special or unusual requirements or conditions in a job that add to the difficulty of the work but are not adequately considered by the other factors, i.e., unusual physical effort, mental concentration or environmental impact on the work. Factors I through IV should provide adequate means for evaluating most positions; therefore, only atypical positions should be assigned values under this factor.

The five factors selected and their subelements were found to be appropriate for evaluation purposes and produce satisfactory results.

Rating scales were developed for each factor to show the various observable levels within each factor and the interrelationship among closely related or dependent elements. The level definitions in the scales are structured to provide equal differences between successive levels.

Selecting Benchmark Positions

Initially, 152 jobs were selected as tentative benchmark positions to be used in developing APTES. The considerations in their selection were that the:

   --position is in an occupation which stands out in the total job population;

   --job is common throughout much of the Government or is important to a major phase of Government activity;

   --duties can be clearly defined;

   --job is broadly related to other occupations;

   --Civil Service Commission had published standards;

   --job is covered in the PATC or BLS salary surveys.

The class series from which these initial benchmark positions were selected represent 51% of the total job population in the APTES category. Some additions and deletions were made in the original list based on the experience of the writers in preparing definitions for each of the jobs selected. These descriptions followed a uniform format; i.e., a brief summary of the principal duties followed by descriptive data outlining each factor. The tentative factor scales were available during the process of description writing. This permitted the writer to assure that the descriptions provided the job data needed to apply the rating scales. (The package of benchmarks for the model system includes 118 positions.)

Ranking and Application of Tentative Rating Scales to Benchmark Positions

In order to establish a base line for development of the ranking system, and also to better identify anomalies in the existing occupational relationships, a six-man panel was selected to rank a smaller sample of 48 jobs from the initial list of benchmark positions according to level of difficulty and responsibility of work. To this sample was added two jobs at overlapping levels from the COMOT benchmarks. The APTES benchmarks selected were for occupational series with populations representing about 40% of the total.

The paired-comparison method was used in ranking the sample of benchmark jobs, first in terms of each factor and then on a whole job basis. The rater following this technique compares each job with each other job by pairing the jobs with each other. This technique makes it possible to compare two jobs without being influenced by the remaining jobs. The pertinent literature and textbooks suggest that under this technique the:

--rankings are individually simpler;

--assumptive bias is reduced significantly;

--results are likely to be reproducible.

The panel members were then given a set of tentative rating scales and asked to apply them to the benchmark positions. The results of these ratings, along with the rankings described above, provided basic data essential to the development of the system including the firming up of the preliminary identification of levels within each factor element.

Developing Point Values and Factor Weights

Upon completion of the factor scale definitions, a system of appropriate factor weights and point values was established.

It is evident that each factor need not have equal weight or significance in measuring the relative worth of work.

Factor weights were obtained by systematically testing possible combinations of factor weights until the combination was identified which produced an acceptable rank order of the tentative benchmark positions in comparison. The weights used in the COMOT system produced a satisfactory relationship. The weights are:

APTES Factor	COMOT Factor	Assigned Weight	Factor Weight Expressed as a Percentage of Total
I	I)	2	20%
II	I)	2	20%
III	II	4	40%
IV	III	1.5	15%
V	IV	.5	5%

Each level in each factor was assigned a point value which is a multiple of ten. For example, the lowest level in Factor I has a value of 20 (2 x 10) and the highest level has a value of 160 (16 x 10). The actual number of levels in Factor V has yet to be determined. (See discussion in the guide chart for Factor V.) A minimum score of 10 was established to discourage its use in evaluating minor job differences. An arbitrary 20 point maximum was established. The factor scale values are:

Factor Scale Values

Factor	Step Values							
	1	2	3	4	5	6	7	8
I	20	40	60	80	100	120	140	160
II	20	40	60	80	100	120	140	160
III	40	80	120	160	200	240	280	320
IV	15	30	45	60	75			
V	(10 to 20 range)							

Developing the Skill Level Structure

All of the tentative benchmark positions were rated according to the factor rating scales as thus weighted. The positions were then placed into groups or "skill levels" by judgmentally considering two characteristics:

--the similarity in point value and hence in level of difficulty and responsibility; and

--the pay relatives for each position.

The objective of the grouping was to achieve pay differences proportioned to work differences for positions and occupations in the APTES category.

A table was then constructed to convert the total point score for any position to an appropriate skill level. The table provides a consistently wider range of points for each higher level of skill, thereby reflecting typical patterns of pay differences and also the broader range of work in successively higher levels of jobs.

Provision for Trainee Positions

The evaluation of truly trainee positions on the basis of duties and responsibilities is always difficult and becomes especially controversial when trainee positions are placed in the same skill levels used for other types of productive workers. APTES proposes to avoid this problem by not placing trainee positions into skill levels. Rather, trainee positions will merely be paid a salary which will be a percentage of the entry salary for the first target position for which the employee is being trained. The exact pay for the trainee can be made proportional to his relative skill and the amount of training needed.

For example, the lowest productive level for an engineer would be Level V. The training level salary for a recent graduate engineer would be based on a percentage of the salary for Level V. Upon satisfactory completion of training, the engineer would move to Level V.

EVALUATION SYSTEM

for

ADMINISTRATIVE, PROFESSIONAL, AND TECHNOLOGICAL POSITIONS

Following is a model for a position evaluation system applicable to nonsupervisory administrative, professional, and technological positions of the Federal Government. This is a factor ranking type of evaluation system using both benchmark position descriptions and factor rating scales. It provides six skill levels, exclusive of purely trainee positions. Trainee positions under this system are not classified into skill levels, but rather are paid a percentage of the salary for the skill level of the lowest productive position in the occupation for which the employee is being trained. For example, the lowest productive level for an engineer would be Level V. The training level salary for a recent graduate engineer would be based on a percentage of the salary for Level V. Upon satisfactory completion of training, the engineer would move to Level V.

Use of Rating Scales

The _first step_ in the evaluation of a position is to compare the position with related benchmark job descriptions and with rating scales, (the benchmark positions further define and clarify the scales) to identify the step which best fits the job being rated. Record the point score for that step. No point scores may be assigned other than those on each factor chart. The reason for this is that the point value assigned to each step on each factor scale represents a _range_ of jobs. Note, for example, that each Index of Benchmark Positions by Factor shows a number and variety of positions for individual factor steps. Since the point values provided on the several factor scales encompass all of the possible job levels that are within the scope of the total scale, no intermediate point values can be interpolated.

Every job should have a point score on each Factor I through IV. Additional points may be assigned under Factor V when certain very unusual circumstances exist. The point scores are recorded and the factor score totaled. This total score represents the relative value of this position and is used to assign individual positions to Levels by applying the conversion table.

Use of Benchmarks

Accompanying the factor rating scales are a number of "benchmark" positions. The evaluations of these benchmarks and the additions to be developed later serve as standards or guidelines for the proper interpretation and application of the rating scales to other positions. By study and analysis of the benchmark positions evaluated at various of the steps of the factor scales and by comparison of the scales with the position being evaluated, the rater can make an appropriate scoring of a position.

Benchmark positions are not provided for each score in each factor. The absence of a benchmark position to illustrate a specific step does not restrict the use of that level of the factor rating scale. Eventually all levels will be backed up with appropriate benchmarks.

Mixed Duty Positions

In point scoring a position which involves the performance of work in two or more occupations, or more than one level in the same occupation, each factor is evaluated on the basis of a study of the individual duties. The evaluator should take into account duties that are significant in terms of the overall purpose of the position and are performed on a recurring basis. Normally, the highest level significant duty controls the determination of the factor score.

Conversion Table

After the position has been rated on each factor rating scale, the scores are totaled and converted to the appropriate level for the position in accordance with the conversion table.

General Instructions

As with all other job evaluation systems, successful application of this factor ranking point rating system depends on understanding of the work being rated, its relationship to other jobs, and sound judgment in the application of the rating scales. The standard "do's" and "don't's" are applicable to this system also; i.e., evaluate the position, not the employee; work from a complete and accurate job description; etc.

FACTOR I. JOB REQUIREMENTS

This factor measures the nature and extent and the level of knowledge and abilities needed to perform work acceptably.

Nature and Extent of Knowledge / Level of Knowledge and Abilities Required	1. Practical knowledge of practices, rules, regulations, theories, principles or techniques developed through on-the-job training and extended experience.	2. Specialized knowledge of pragmatic and theoretical principles and practices developed through on-the-job training and relevant experience typically after baccalaureate education.	3. Broad knowledge of the principles, theories, and practices of a recognized profession, developed through a baccalaureate or higher education plus relevant experience and training.
A. Standard methods, practices, and procedures of a discipline or specialized field and the body of facts relevant to the assigned categories of work.	20	40	60
B. Elementary principles, theories, and methodology or advanced methods, practices, and procedures.	40	60	80
C. Full range of generally accepted and commonly used principles, theories, methodology, and precedents.	60	80	100
D. Advanced theories, principles, methodology, and new developments.	80	100	120
E. Mastery of field plus ability to cope with unprecedented types of problems by extending accepted methods and techniques or developing new ones.		120	140
F. Mastery of field plus ability to generate new hypotheses or principles or to extend the accepted principles, theories, or concepts beyond their previously recognized limits.		140	160

FACTOR II. DIFFICULTY OF WORK

This factor measures the complexity or intricacy of work and the mental demands, i.e., judgment, originality, and other mental effort required, as affected by the quality and relevance of the available guidelines.*

Nature of Guidelines (Mental Demands) / Complexity of Assigned Work	4. Numerous, prescribed, well established, and directly applicable, and can be readily selected. Judgment is limited to relating guidelines to specific case. In analytical work, answers are logically and readily obtained.	5. Generally accepted but are not always clearly applicable. Judgment is needed in selecting the most pertinent guidelines, in interpreting precedents, and in adapting standard formulas, methods, or procedures to fit facts and conditions.	6. Generally applicable but ambiguous or only partially relevant or otherwise seriously deficient. Judgment is needed in extensively adapting or in making significant compromises to fit unusual or complex situations.	7. Obscure, nonexistent, irrelevant or contradictory for major parts of work. Creativity and ingenuity are needed to devise new approaches to deal with previously unsolved or novel problems.
G. Repetitive, restricted in scope and intricacy; involving few variables.	20	40		
H. Repetitive, restricted in scope but of substantial intricacy, involving several variables or considerations with interrelationships that are not clearly evident.	40	60		
J. Broad in scope and of substantial intricacy involving many variables or considerations with interrelationships difficult to ascertain, and usually having conflicting aspects requiring individual and differential diagnosis and treatment.		80	100	120
K. Broad in scope and of great intricacy involving many complex and significant variables or considerations which are new, either in basic character or in the circumstances or situations in which they occur.		100	120	140
L. In addition to being broad in scope, of great intricacy, and of a new and unprecedented nature, also require study and consideration of the impact of alternative possible solutions on other major programs, situations, organizations, or future developments.			140	160

* The term "guidelines" here means all types of source materials including references, manuals, precedents, oral and written instructions, textbooks, standard methods, and procedures, etc.

FACTOR III. RESPONSIBILITY

This measures the assistance and control provided by the supervisor and the impact of work on the accomplishment of the mission of the organization.

Impact of Work / Supervisory Participation and Control	8. Application of standardized or accepted practice, usually in connection with individual cases, persons, or situations.	9. Substantial contribution involving nonroutine decisions and recommendations based on agency guidelines and policies.	10. Major contribution involving authoritative application of agency policy and practice to especially complex or important matters.	11. Extensive and consequential contribution involving support, development or recommendation of major objectives, policies, programs, or practices.
M. Specific instruction on new types of assignments. Work occasionally checked in process. All work reviewed for adherence to instructions and guidelines, soundness of judgment and conclusions, and accuracy.	40			
N. Purpose and desired results indicated, and anticipated unusual problems discussed. Deviations from guidelines must be referred to the supervisor. Case actions or recurring work clearly covered by guidelines may or may not be reviewed. Otherwise, work reviewed for adherence to instructions, soundness of judgment and conclusions, technical adequacy, accuracy, and conformance with practice or precedent.	80	120		
P. Purpose and desired results indicated. Unusual problems, proposed deviations from guidelines or practice discussed at the discretion of the employee. Case actions, recurring work (even where there is some variety or departure from standard guidelines) may or may not be reviewed. Otherwise, work reviewed for soundness of judgment and conclusions, general technical adequacy, and conformance with practice and policy.	120	160	200	240
Q. General objectives and boundaries indicated. Problems during work raising questions about objectives and boundaries are discussed. Technical instruction neither sought nor needed. Decisions and recommendations (other than on individual cases) are reviewed for attainment of objectives and compliance with agency policy.		200	240	280
R. Assignments are usually planned with the supervisor in terms of general objectives and boundaries. Problems arising during the work which may have a possible impact on agency policy are discussed. Decisions and recommendations are reviewed for overall accomplishment and impact upon agency mission, policy, or practice.		240	280	320

FACTOR IV. PERSONAL RELATIONSHIPS

This measures the skill required in work relationships with others and the importance of such relationships to the success of the work.

Nature and Purpose / Scope of Work Contacts	12. Persons in the same agency.	13. Persons employed by other agencies, or with the public.	14. Persons, officials, or representatives of organizations which have an unusually significant impact on the programs or policies involved in the work.
S. Cooperative work relationships incidental to purpose of the work involving giving and receiving factual information about the work.	15	30	45
T. Explanation or interpretation to render service, carry out policies, or maintain coordination.	30	45	60
U. Nonroutine, cooperative problem solving requiring discussion and persuasion to gain concurrence or cooperation in the face of significant difference of opinion or controversy.	45	60	75

NOTE: Personal contacts are not evaluated above the S-12 level if the contacts occur only infrequently or irregularly, or are not an essential aspect of the main purpose and nature of the position, or for other reasons are only incidental to the duties and responsibilities of the position.

FACTOR V.   OTHER REQUIREMENTS

This measures any special or unusual requirements or conditions in a job that add to the difficulty of the work but are not adequately considered by the other factors.   Examples of conditions that may warrant consideration are jobs which involve:

        --an unusual degree of physical effort;
        --an unusual degree of required mental effort or concentration;
        --an unusual degree of environmental impact on the work.

Factors I through IV should provide adequate means for evaluating most positions; therefore, only atypical positions in the APTES category should be assigned values under this factor.   Where an agency deems it appropriate to assign such values to specific positions, the circumstances and appropriate point value must be clearly expressed in the pertinent agency benchmark job descriptions.   Since the factor is applicable in only unusual cases, no benchmark positions included in the initial group of proposed Government-wide descriptions provide for credit under Factor V.

In those unusual positions where credit under this factor is appropriate, point values are restricted to a 10-20 point range.   Intermediate scores must be in increments of five points and scaled in proportion to the added difficulty. The maximum "add-on" for this factor under any one or any combination of elements is 20 points.

CAUTION -- Care must be exercised not to add on values for Factor V when the identified condition in fact involves additional "know-how" which can and should be recognized under Factor I.

             Care also must be exercised to avoid adding values for elements that are not appropriately evaluated under a job ranking system. For example, the risk involved in working in a hazardous environment can best be evaluated and compensated for on a pay differential basis.   The amount of pay differential should be based on the degree of risk.   However, if the presence of a hazard requires additional knowledges, job skills, or responsibilities, these should be recognized and evaluated under the four basic factors.

CONVERSION TABLE

Point Score Range	Skill Level
620 - 735	I
505 - 615	II
395 - 500	III
290 - 390	IV
190 - 285	V
95 - 185	VI

All trainee positions with point values <u>below</u> the minimum required for the productive or minimum Level for the specific occupation. The Trainee Salary Rate is a prescribed percentage of the salary for the Level of position for which the employee is being trained.	TL

LIBRARY EDUCATION AND MANPOWER

*A Statement of Policy Adopted by the Council of
the American Library Association, June 30, 1970* *

1 The purpose of the policy statement is to recommend categories of library manpower, and levels of training and education appropriate to the preparation of personnel for these categories, which will support the highest standards of library service for all kinds of libraries and the most effective use of the variety of manpower skills and qualifications needed to provide it.

2 Library service as here understood is concerned with knowledge and information in their several forms—their identification, selection, acquisition, preservation, organization, communication and interpretation, and with assistance in their use.

3 To meet the goals of library service, both professional and supportive staff are needed in libraries. Thus the library occupation is much broader than that segment of it which is the library profession, but the library profession has responsibility for defining the training and education required for the preparation of personnel who work in libraries at any level, supportive or professional.

4 Skills other than those of librarianship may also have an important contribution to make to the achievement of superior library service. There should be equal recognition in both the professional and supportive ranks for those individuals whose expertise contributes to the effective performance of the library.

5 A constant effort must be made to promote the most effective utilization of manpower at all levels, both professional and supportive. The tables on page 2 (Figure 1) suggest a set of categories which illustrate a means for achieving this end.

* Throughout this statement, wherever the term "librarianship" is used, it is meant to be read in its broadest sense as encompassing the relevant concepts of information science and documentation; wherever the term "libraries" is used, the current models of media centers, learning centers, educational resources centers, information, documentation, and referral centers are also assumed. To avoid the necessity of repeating the entire gamut of variations and expansions, the traditional library terminology is employed in its most inclusive meaning.

Figure 1

CATEGORIES OF LIBRARY PERSONNEL—PROFESSIONAL

TITLE For positions requiring:		BASIC REQUIREMENTS	NATURE OF RESPONSIBILITY
library-related qualifications	nonlibrary-related qualifications		
Senior Librarian	Senior Specialist	In addition to relevant experience, education beyond the M.A. [i.e., a master's degree in any of its variant designations: M.A., M.L.S., M.S.L.S., M.Ed., etc.] as: post-master's degree; Ph.D.; relevant continuing education in many forms	Top-level responsibilities, including but not limited to administration; superior knowledge of some aspect of librarianship, or of other subject fields of value to the library
Librarian	Specialist	Master's degree	Professional responsibilities including those of management, which require independent judgment, interpretation of rules and procedures, analysis of library problems, and formulation of original and creative solutions for them (normally utilizing knowledge of the subject field represented by the academic degree)

CATEGORIES OF LIBRARY PERSONNEL—SUPPORTIVE

TITLE		BASIC REQUIREMENTS	NATURE OF RESPONSIBILITY
Library Associate	Associate Specialist	Bachelor's degree (with or without course work in library science); OR bachelor's degree, plus additional academic work short of the master's degree (in librarianship for the Library Associate; in other relevant subject fields for the Associate Specialist)	Supportive responsibilities at a high level, normally working within the established procedures and techniques, and with some supervision by a professional, but requiring judgment, and subject knowledge such as is represented by a full, four-year college education culminating in the bachelor's degree
Library Technical Assistant	Technical Assistant	At least two years of college-level study; OR A.A. degree, with or without Library Technical Assistant training; OR post-secondary school training in relevant skills	Tasks performed as supportive staff to Associates and higher ranks, following established rules and procedures, and including, at the top level, supervision of such tasks
Clerk		Business school or commercial courses, supplemented by in-service training or on-the-job experience	Clerical assignments as required by the individual library

6 The titles recommended here represent categories or broad classifications, within which it is assumed that there will be several levels of promotional steps. Specific job titles may be used within any category: for example, catalogers, reference librarians, children's librarians would be included in either the "Librarian" or (depending upon the level of their responsibilities and qualifications) "Senior Librarian" categories; department heads, the director of the library, and certain specialists would presumably have the additional qualifications and responsibilities which place them in the "Senior Librarian" category.

7 Where specific job titles dictated by local usage and tradition do not make clear the level of the staff member's qualification and responsibility, it is recommended that reference to the ALA category title be used parenthetically to provide the clarification desirable for communication and reciprocity. For example:

REFERENCE ASSISTANT (Librarian)   HEAD CATALOGER (Senior Librarian)

LIBRARY AIDE (Library Technical Assistant)

8 The title "Librarian" carries with it the connotation of "professional" in the sense that professional tasks are those which require a special background and education on the basis of which library needs are identified, problems are analyzed, goals are set, and original and creative solutions are formulated for them, integrating theory into practice, and planning, organizing, communicating, and administering successful programs of service to users of the library's materials and services. In defining services to users, the professional person recognizes potential users as well as current ones, and designs services which will reach all who could benefit from them.

9 The title "Librarian" therefore should be used only to designate positions in libraries which utilize the qualifications and impose the responsibilities suggested above. Positions which are primarily devoted to the routine application of established rules and techniques, however useful and essential to the effective operation of a library's ongoing services, should not carry the word "Librarian" in the job title.

10 It is recognized that every type and size of library may not need staff appointments in each of these categories. It is urged, however, that this basic scheme be introduced wherever possible to permit where needed the necessary flexibility in staffing.

11 The salaries for each category should offer a range of promotional steps sufficient to permit a career-in-rank. The top salary in any category should overlap the beginning salary in the next higher category, in order to give recognition to the value of experience and knowledge gained on the job.

12 Inadequately supported libraries or libraries too small to be able to afford professional staff should nevertheless have access to the services and supervision of a librarian. To obtain the professional guidance that they themselves cannot supply, such libraries should promote cooperative arrangements or join larger systems of cooperating libraries through which supervisory personnel can be supported. Smaller libraries which are part of such a system can often maintain the local service with building staff at the Associate level.

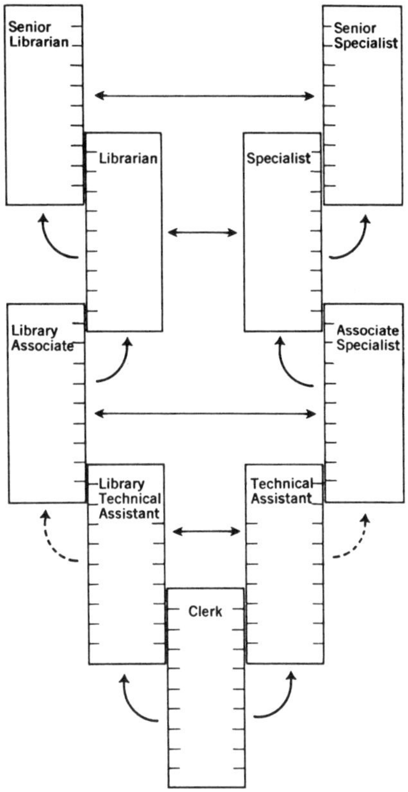

Figure 2

If one thinks of Career *Lattices* rather than Career *Ladders*, the flexibility intended by the Policy Statement may be better visualized. The movement among staff responsibilities, for example, is not necessarily directly up, but often may be lateral to increased responsibilities of equal importance. Each category embodies a number of promotional steps within it, as indicated by the gradation markings on each bar. The top of any category overlaps in responsibility and salary the next higher category.

Comments on the Categories

13 The *Clerk* classifications do not require formal academic training in library subjects. The assignments in these categories are based upon general clerical and secretarial proficiencies. Familiarity with basic library terminology and routines necessary to adapt clerical skills to the library's needs is best learned on the job.

14 The *Technical Assistant* categories assume certain kinds of specific "technical" skills; they are not meant simply to accommodate advanced clerks. While clerical skills might well be part of a Technical Assistant's equipment, the emphasis in his assignment should be on the special technical skill. For example, someone who is skilled in handling audiovisual equipment, or at introductory data processing, or in making posters and other displays might well be hired in the Technical Assistant category for these skills, related to librarianship only to the extent that they are employed in a library. A *Library*

Technical Assistant is a person with certain specifically library-related skills—in preliminary bibliographic searching for example, or utilization of certain mechanical equipment—the performance of whose duties seldom requires him to call upon a background in general education.

15 The *Associate* categories assume a need for an educational background like that represented by a bachelor's degree from a good four-year institution of higher education in the United States. Assignments may be such that library knowledge is less important than general education, and whether the title is *Library* Associate or Associate *Specialist* depends upon the nature of the tasks and responsibilities assigned. Persons holding the B.A. degree, with or without a library science minor or practical experience in libraries, are eligible for employment in this category. The title within the Associate category that is assigned to the individual will depend upon the relevance of his training and background to the specific assignment.

16 The Associate category also provides the opportunity for persons of promise and exceptional talent to begin library employment below the level of professional (as defined in this statement) and thus to combine employment in a library with course work at the graduate level. Where this kind of work/study arrangement is made, the combination of work and formal study should provide 1) increasing responsibility within the Associate ranks as the individual moves through the academic program, and 2) eligibility for promotion, upon completion of the master's degree, to positions of professional responsibility and attendant reclassification to the professional category.

17 The first professional category—*Librarian, or Specialist*—assumes responsibilities that are professional in the sense described in paragraph #8 above. A good liberal education plus graduate-level study in the field of specialization (either in librarianship or in a relevant field) are seen as the minimum preparation for the kinds of assignments implied. The title, however, is given for a position entailing professional responsibilities and not automatically upon achievement of the academic degree.

18 The *Senior* categories assume relevant professional experience as well as qualifications beyond those required for admission to the first professional ranks. Normally it is assumed that such advanced qualifications shall be held in some specialty, either in a particular aspect of librarianship or some relevant subject field. Subject specializations are as applicable in the *Senior Librarian* category as they are in the *Senior Specialist* category.

19 Administrative responsibilities entail advanced knowledge and skills comparable to those represented by any other high-level specialty, and appointment to positions in top administration should normally require the qualifications of a *Senior Librarian* with a specialization in administration. This category, however, is not limited to administrators, whose specialty is only one of several specializations of value to the library service. There are many areas of special knowledge within librarianship which are equally important and to which equal recognition in prestige and salary should be given. A highly qualified person with a specialist responsibility in some aspect of librarianship—archives, bibliography, reference, for example—should be eligible for advanced status and financial rewards without being forced to abandon for administrative responsibilities his area of major competence.

Implications for Formal Education

20 Until examinations are identified that are valid and reliable tests of equivalent qualifications, the academic degree (or evidence of years of academic work completed) is recommended as the single best means for determining that an applicant has the background recommended for each category.

21 In the selection of applicants for positions at any level, and for admission to library schools, attention should be paid to personal aptitudes and qualifications in addition to academic ones. The nature of the position or specialty, and particularly the degree to which it entails working with others, with the public, or with special audiences or materials should be taken into account in the evaluation of a prospective student or employee.

22 As library services change and expand, as new audiences are reached, as new media take on greater importance in the communication process, and as new approaches to the handling of materials are introduced, the kinds of preparation required of those who will be employed in libraries will become more varied. Degrees in fields other than librarianship will be needed in the Specialist categories. For many Senior Librarian positions, an advanced degree in another subject field rather than an additional degree in librarianship, may be desirable. Previous experience need not always have been in libraries to have pertinence for appointment in a library.

23 Because the principles of librarianship are applied to the materials of information and knowledge broader than any single field, and because they are related to subject matter outside of librarianship itself, responsible education in these principles should be built upon a broad rather than a narrowly specialized background education. To the extent that courses in library science are introduced in the four-year, undergraduate program, they should be concentrated in the last two years and should not constitute a major inroad into course work in the basic disciplines: the humanities, the sciences, and the social sciences.

24 Training courses for Library Technical Assistants at the junior or community college level should be recognized as essentially terminal in intent (or as service courses rather than a formal program of education), designed for the preparation of supportive rather than professional staff. Students interested in librarianship as a career should be counselled to take the general four-year college course rather than the specific two-year program, with its inevitable loss of time and transferable content. Graduates of the two-year programs are not prohibited from taking the additional work leading to the bachelor's and master's degrees, provided they demonstrate the necessary qualifications for admission to the senior college program, but it is an indirect and less desirable way to prepare for a professional career, and the student should be so informed.

25 Emphasis in the two-year Technical Assistant programs should be more on skills training than on general library concepts and procedures. In many cases it would be better from the standpoint of the student to pursue more broadly-based vocational courses which will teach technical skills applicable in a variety of job situations rather than those limited solely to the library setting.

26 Undergraduate instruction in library science other than training courses for Library Technical Assistants should be primarily a contribution to liberal education rather than an opportunity to provide technological and methodological training. This does not preclude the inclusion of course work related to the basic skills of library practice, but it does affect teaching method and approach, and implies an emphasis on the principles that underlie practice rather than how-to-do-it, vocational training.

27 Certain practical skills and procedures at all levels are best learned on the job rather than in the academic classroom. These relate typically to details of operation which may vary from institution to institution, or to routines which require repetition and practice for their mastery. The responsibility for such in-service parts of the total preparation of both librarians and supportive staff rests with libraries and library systems rather than with the library schools.

28 The objective of the master's programs in librarianship should be to prepare librarians capable of anticipating and engineering the change and improvement required to move the profession constantly forward. The curriculum and teaching methods should be designed to serve this kind of education for the future rather than to train for the practice of the present.

29 Certain interdisciplinary concepts (information science is an example) are so intimately related to the basic concepts underlying library service that they properly become a part of the library school curriculum rather than simply an outside specialty. Where such content is introduced into the

library school it should be incorporated into the entire curriculum, enriching every course where it is pertinent. The stop-gap addition of individual courses in such a specialty, not integrated into the program as a whole, is an inadequate assimilation of the intellectual contribution of the new concept to library education and thinking.

30 In recognition of the many areas of related subject matter of importance to library service, library schools should make knowledge in other fields readily available to students, either through the appointment of staff members from other disciplines or through permitting students to cross departmental, divisional, and institutional lines in reasoned programs in related fields. Intensive specializations at the graduate level, building upon strengths in the parent institution or the community, are a logical development in professional library education.

31 Library schools should be encouraged to experiment with new teaching methods, new learning devices, different patterns of scheduling and sequence, and other means, both traditional and nontraditional, that may increase the effectiveness of the students' educational experience.

32 Research has an important role to play in the educational process as a source of new knowledge both for the field of librarianship in general and for library education in particular. In its planning, budgeting, and organizational design, the library school should recognize research, both theoretical and applied, as an imperative responsibility.

Continuing Education

33 Continuing Education is essential for all library personnel, professional and supportive, whether they remain within a position category or are preparing to move into a higher one. Continuing education opportunities include both formal and informal learning situations, and need not be limited to library subjects or the offerings of library schools.

34 The "continuing education" which leads to eligibility for Senior Librarian or Specialist positions may take any of the forms suggested directly above so long as the additional education and experience are relevant to the responsibilities of the assignment.

35 Library administrators must accept responsibility for providing support and opportunities (in the form of leaves, sabbaticals, and released time) for the continuing education of their staffs.

Additional copies available from

Office for Library Education
American Library Association
50 E. Huron St., Chicago, Ill. 60611

Illinois Library Task Analysis Project
Phase II: Study of Public Library Tasks

Objectives of the Study

The primary objective of this study was to test the validity of the ALA
policy statement on <u>Library Education and Manpower</u> by applying it to the tasks
described in Phase I of the Illinois Task Analysis Project. A model was to be
developed in which the tasks would be arranged in accordance with the definitions
established in the policy statement, on the basis of the consultant's experience
and judgment and bearing in mind the scaling of all appropriate factors by SERD
(Social, Educational Research and Development, Inc.). This would be the exact process which would have to be followed by an administrator attempting to apply the
new manpower policy in an individual library, and the result, besides serving as a
test of the policy's validity, should also serve as a demonstration to administrators
of how to make such application to positions in their own libraries.

Only public libraries were to be included in the study, and this was inter-
preted to include the State library agency, the processing center, and the system
headquarters, as well as the individual public libraries included in Phase I of the
project.

Formal job descriptions were not to be produced, since any such grouping
of tasks into positions would involve knowing the quantity of such work to be
performed in a given library or organizational unit, and this information was not
available. Promotional lines from one grouping or level of tasks to another were
to be indicated, however, since this is a major element in the manpower policy.

Methodology

Substantial and detailed review was made of the 1615 tasks described in
Phase I of the project by SERD, and of their coding of the tasks by Functional Areas,
General and Specific Tasks, and the scales of Performance Standards (II),

Task Environment (III), Worker Functions (IV), General Educational Development (V),
Worker Instructions (VI), Training Time (VII), Time to Complete the Task (VIII),
and Extraordinary Physical Demands (IX).

Two of the scales were ruled out at the very beginning as not having
significant validity for the study: VIII - Time to Complete the Task, and IX -
Extraordinary Physical Demands. The coding of General and Specific Tasks was not
formally used, since the distinction was apparent from a reading of the tasks.
It should be noted, however, that for the kind of task analysis attempted in
Phase I, only specific tasks can be of use. The inclusion of so-called "general"
tasks, actually clusters of tasks, contradicts the expressed objective of the
analysis attempted. For reasons of practicality, however, both general and specific
tasks were used in this study, with the breakdown of general into specific "assumed,"
or supplied without formally setting it down, on the basis of the analyst's experience with the duties as performed.

Two of the most important codings were not supplied: that listed in SERD's
report as Scale X - Knowledge/Skills/Abilities, and the type of library in which the
task occurred. For a study to be based entirely and reliably on the findings of
Phase I, the Knowledge/Skills/Abilities factor is an absolute essential. In order
to perform the study, it again had to be supplied, implicitly, from the analyst's
experience. The absence of coding by type of library does not in any way affect
the validity of the study, but the need to sort out all the tasks occurring only in
school, college and university, or special libraries, added a great deal of unneces-
sary work and had serious impact on the useability of the machine runs.

It was apparent from the first line-by-line study of the tasks ordered by
Training Requirements that there was going to be significant disagreement with SERD's

scoring, based largely on the missing Knowledge/Skills/Abilities factor, and also
that a rather high proportion of the tasks were either duplicates or would be unuseable because of the ambiguity of their description. These problems, combined
with the inability to sort by type of library, meant that any machine sort of the
data would be not only cumbersome because of the inclusion each time of tasks in all
types of libraries, but highly unreliable unless the scoring of all the scales were
first reviewed, reevaluated, recoded and rerun.

It was therefore determined that the study would be based on a manual sort
of the cards, with duplicates, unuseable descriptions, and tasks specifically identified or occurring solely in school, college/university, and special libraries excluded, and with ratings for individual tasks reappraised at each stage of their use.

Procedure and Findings

The first step was to eliminate from the 1615 tasks those not to be included in the study. Two hundred eighty-five (285) tasks were sorted out as specifically identified or occurring solely in school libraries, 164 as specifically identified or occurring solely in college/university libraries, and 70 as specifically
identified or occurring solely in special libraries. Tasks identified or recognizable as occurring in the State library, processing center, and system headquarters
were included in the study without separate treatment.

There was a fair number of tasks which could be either school or college/
university, or both. The decision between the two was made arbitrarily, usually on
the basis of vocabulary, but the resulting count may not be precise.

Ninety-five (95) tasks were eliminated as duplicates in this or subsequent
sorts, and 114 as being unuseable. It may be useful to see examples of some occurring in the latter category. Most were determined to be unuseable because of

ambiguity or vagueness of description, which made it impossible to determine what the nature of the task really was; for example,

> Determines records to be kept in public library

> Provides technical assistance in non-professional areas to libraries in the system

> Reviews and evaluates staff studies and revises or implements results

> Approves proposals for new programs.

Others were simply not "tasks" by any definition, as

> Maintains working climate conducive to staff morale and patron needs

> Anticipates new problems and needs for library and develops programs dealing with problems before critical situations arise.

In the case of duplicates, the most specific or the most clearly stated version was retained.

Duplicate and unuseable tasks were not culled from those identified as belonging in excluded types of libraries.

This left 840 tasks as the universe of the study -- those occurring in the public library, including State agency, system headquarters, and processing center. Obviously many of these tasks are universal in libraries, occurring also in other types of libraries.

These tasks were then sorted into ten categories -- the nine established in the ALA policy statement on Education and Manpower and a tenth called, tentatively, "Custodial-Maintenance and others not included by definition in the statement."

1   Clerk

2   Library Technical Assistant

3   Technical Assistant

4   Library Associate

5   Associate Specialist

6   Librarian

7   Specialist

8   Senior Librarian

9   Senior Specialist

0   Custodial-Maintenance and Others

It rapidly became apparent that a number of additional categories would need to be inserted for sorting purposes. One was called Supervisory Clerical (as distinct from Library Technical Assistant). Another consisted of administrative or supervisory tasks which were multi-level, depending on where they occurred in the organization, as

Approves vacation and leave requests of staff

Makes annual evaluation of staff members

Conducts monthly staff meetings

Writes annual report of activities in department.

This group was ultimately eliminated from the study since they were un-placeable by category. Their existence should not be forgotten, however, in any further use of the task descriptions, since they are important elements of positions at several different levels.

A separate category was established for Audio-Visual in the first sort, but this was later eliminated and the tasks within it sorted by Functional Area and integrated with the others in the study.

A small category of self-development items was also separated out in the first sort, but later integrated or, in a few cases, excluded from the study.

Also separated in the first sort were a few tasks involving the transfer of work at the conclusion of a process. SERD viewed this transfer as a clerical operation, but in almost all cases it was simply a matter of the person who had performed the preceding step passing the work on to the next person, and these tasks were later integrated into the main body of the tasks with interpretation and evaluation based on the task which had just been completed.

Categories were also set up for Librarian or Specialist, Senior Librarian or Senior Specialist, and these were retained, since the tasks could appropriately be performed by either, depending on the staff-utilization pattern of the library. One was also inserted for Associate Specialist or Specialist, consisting largely of tasks which could be delegated by the Specialist to an assistant if the unit were large enough to justify a second position.

"Other" was found to consist of custodial-maintenance, truck or mobile-unit driver, and shipping room functions. Since tasks of this nature were not included in the policy statement, no further analysis was made of them.

Within most of the categories, the tasks were then sorted by Functional Area. This provides a good example of why a machine-sort based on SERD's codings would not be reliable. More than a third of the Clerical tasks allocated by SERD to Functional Area 2 (Selection and Acquisition) needed to be changed, most of them to 1 (Administration) or to 3 (Cataloging and Processing), or in some cases to 4 (Registration and Circulation). At this stage numerous additions were made to the Unuseable category (but included in the total given earlier) because of such problems as not being able to tell when "orders" referred to books or other media and when to supplies or equipment.

Similarly, about one-fourth of the Clerical tasks coded 3 were changed, and again duplicates became visible which had not been caught in the first sorting.

In Category 4 (Registration and Circulation) the problem arose of having tasks described involving several different kinds of charging systems. They were all left in, with the result that considerable duplication remains. There was much confusion in the placement of Interlibrary Loan functions, with SERD placing some in Category IV and some in Category VI - Reader Services. While either could be defended, they were all placed in Circulation for the sake of consistency.

Within several of the Functional Areas, with large numbers of tasks, sub-divisions were established, as

Clerical: FA 1 (Administration)

Unskilled Clerical

Simple Machine Operation

Typing

Secretarial

Switchboard

Supplies

Personnel and Payroll

Fiscal

Clerical: FA 3 (Cataloging and Processing)

General Processing

Newspaper Processing

Physical Preparation

Clerical: FA 4 (Registration and Circulation)

Registration

Circulation

Overdues/Fines

Shelving

Reserves

Interlibrary Loan

The Technical Assistant category, although small enough numerically that it was not sorted by Functional Area, was divided in order better to see its composition, e.g.

Audio-visual Equipment

Data Processing

Microfilming

Printing

Photography

Other

Similarly, Specialist was divided into:

General Management

Personnel

Public Relations

Computer

Audio-Visual

No tasks were placed in the Senior Specialist category, probably a result of the size of the libraries included in the study.

Senior Specialist or Senior Librarian was divided into

Professional

General Management

Buildings/Architecture

Budget/Fiscal.

CHART A   Distribution of Tasks

    School Libraries   285
    College/University Libraries   164
    Special Libraries   70
    Other
      (Custodial-Maintenance, Driver, Shipping
                         Room)   29
    Multi-Level Supervisory   18
    Unuseable   114
    Duplicates   <u>95</u>

          Total <u>not used</u> in study 775

Clerical: FA 1 - <u>Administration</u>
    Unskilled Clerical   11
    Simple Machine Operation   25
    Typist   10
    Secretarial   11
    Switchboard   1
    Supplies   8
    Personnel and Payroll   15
    Fiscal   <u>18</u>

         Total Administration 99

        <u>FA 2</u> - <u>Selection and Acquisition</u> 57

        <u>FA 3</u> - <u>Cataloging and Processing</u>
           General Processing   51
           Newspaper Processing   3
           Physical Preparation   <u>16</u>

        Total Cataloging and Processing 70

        <u>FA 4</u> - <u>Registration and Circulation</u>
           Registration   6
           Circulation   31
           Overdues/Fines   17
           Shelving   13
           Reserves   9
           Interlibrary Loan   <u>21</u>

        Total Registration and Circulation 97

        <u>FA 5</u> - <u>References Services</u> 1

        <u>FA 6</u> - <u>Patron Services</u> 6

        <u>FA 7</u> - <u>Collection Maintenance</u> 27

        <u>FA 8</u> - <u>Facility Maintenance</u> 3

        Total Non-Supervisory Clerical 360

<u>Supervisory Clerical</u>:   27

CHART A - continued

Library Technical Assistant:

FA 1 - Administration 0

FA 2 - Selection and Acquisition 21

FA 3 - Cataloging and Processing 33

FA 4 - Registration and Circulation 3

FA 5 - Reference Services 1

FA 6 - Patron Services 2

FA 7 - Collection Maintenance 11

FA 8 - Facility Maintenance 0

Total Library Technical Assistant 71

Technical Assistant:

Audio-Visual   14
Data Processing   7
Microfilming   5
Printing   5
Photography   4
Other   2

Total Technical Assistant 37

Library Associate: 14

Associate Specialist: 15

Associate Specialist or Specialist: 15

Librarian:

FA 1 - Administration 10

FA 2 - Selection and Acquisition 36

FA 3 - Cataloging and Processing 19

FA 4 - Registration and Circulation 6

FA 5 - Reference Services 5

FA 6 - Patron Services 33

FA 7 - Collection Maintenance 10

FA 8 - Facility Maintenance 0

Total Librarian 119

Specialist:

General Management   8
Personnel   26
Public Relations   18
Computer   8
Audio-Visual   7

Total Specialist 67

CHART A - continued

Librarian or Specialist: 24

Senior Librarian:

    FA 1 - Administration   28
    FA 2 - Selection and Acquisition   8
    FA 3 - Cataloging and Processing   3
    FA 6 - Patron Services   2
    FA's 4,5,7,8   0

          Total Senior Librarian 41

Senior Librarian or Senior Specialist:
    Professional   5
    General Management   19
    Buildings/Architecture   12
    Budget/Fiscal   14

          Total Senior Librarian or
               Senior Specialist 50

          TOTAL - All Tasks Used in Study 840

SUMMARY OF DISTRIBUTION OF TASKS USED IN STUDY

Non-Supervisory Clerical 360
Supervisory Clerical 27
Library Technical Assistant 71
Technical Assistant 37
Library Associate 14
Associate Specialist 15
Associate Specialist or Specialist 15
Librarian 119
Specialist 67
Librarian or Specialist 24
Senior Librarian 41
Senior Librarian or Senior Specialist 50

          TOTAL - All Tasks Used in Study 840

*   *   *

As the next stage of the study the tasks, thus arranged, were reviewed in the light of SERD's scaling of the following factors:

VII - Training Time

V - General Educational Development

A - Reasoning

B - Mathematics (only for those in which it
was likely to be a significant factor)

C - Language

VI - Worker Instructions

II-A Performance Standards - Who or What Sets the Standards

III - Task Environment

The Training Time factor was obviously the most significant in terms of the objectives of the study, and although it was known that the correlation was high between Factors VII and V, General Educational Development (GED) was reviewed simply as a cross-check on SERD's evaluations.

Scale VIII (Time Required to Complete the Task) and IX (Extraordinary Physical Demands) had earlier been eliminated, and Scale V-B (Mathematics) was so obviously not significant in most tasks that it was used only in categories where it seemed likely to be required.

Scale IV (Worker Functions: Data, People, Things) was included experimentally, but the scattering was so widespread that it was meaningless for the purposes of this particular study. This factor would have great importance, however, in actually grouping tasks into jobs, and a careful analysis of it for all the tasks performed in libraries would surely be of interest to those concerned with recruitment and selection of library staff at all levels, and with their educational preparation and on-the-job training and development.

Scale II-B (Quality Required) was excluded because, for the purposes of this particular study, the variation of error permitted was meaningless unless accompanied by a rating of the consequence of error. As illustration, Task 1150, "types multilith masters" and Task 1368, "manages and controls budget, including major expenditures and transfer of budgetary items" are both, accurately, coded 1 - "error-free quality (or _very_, _very_ close to it) is required"; but the difference in level is considerable.

II-C (Are Standards Written or Unwritten?) and II-D (Pace or Productivity) were excluded; again, because they say nothing about level of work or educational requirements.

The codings as listed in Chart B represent the range, or _predominant_ or _characteristic_ valuations, and where one or more occurred with considerably greater frequency than the others listed, these are underlined.

The scalings used here are essentially SERD's. A few changes were made for individual tasks in cases of marked disagreement, but in no instance was the range for a category affected by this.

CHART B

Review of SERD[1]/Scales by Position Categories

Position Categories	Scale VII	Scale V			Scale VI	Scale II-A	Scale III
		A	B	C			
Clerical:							
FA 1 - Administration							
Unskilled Clerical	1-4	1-3	-	1-3	1-2	2-3	2-3
Simple Machine Operation	1-4	1-3	-	1-3	1-2	3	2-3
Typing	4,5	2-3	-	3-4	2	2-3	2-3
Secretarial	3,4,5,6	3-4	-	3-4	1-2	2-3	2-3
Switchboard	3	2	-	3	1	3	2
Supplies	4,5	2-3	-	3-4	2,3,4	2-3	2-3
Personnel and Payroll	3-6	3-4	-	3,4,5	2-4	3	2
Fiscal	4-6	3-4	3-5	3-4	2-4	2-3	3,9,10,12
FA 2 - Selection and Acquisition	1-4	1-4	-	1,2,3,4	1,2,3	2-3	2, 3,12
FA 3 - Cataloging and Processing							
Regular Processing	1-4	1,2,3	-	2,3,4	1-2	2-3	2,12
Newspaper Processing	1-3	1	--	1,2	1	2-3	2
Physical Preparation	1,4	1-4	-	3,5	1-2	2-3	2-3
FA 4 - Registration and Circulation							
Registration	4	2-3	-	3-4	1-4	2,3	2,3,10,12
Circulation	1-4	1-3	-	1,2,3,4	1-4	2,3	1,2,3, 7, 10,12
Overdues/Fines	3,4,5	1-3	-	2-4	1,2,3,4	2,3	2,3,5,8 ,9,12
Shelving	1,3,4	1-3	-	2-3	1,2,3	3	2
Reserves	4	2-3	-	2,3,4	2	3	2
Interlibrary Loan	1-4	1,2,3,4	-	2,3,4	1,2,3	2-3	2-3
FA 5 - Reference Services	4	2	-	3	3	3	4
FA 6 - Patron Services	3-4	1,2,4	-	2,3	1-2	2-3	1-3
FA 7 - Collection Maintenance	1-4	1-3	-	1-3	1-2	2-3	2-3
FA 8 - Facility Maintenance	1-4	1-3	-	3	1,2	2-3	2-3
Supervisory Clerical	5-7	3-4	-	3,4,5	4-6	3	2,4,5,7,9, 10,12

[1]SERD Report gives complete description of scales used.

CHART B - continued

Position Categories	Scale VII	Scale V			Scale VI	Scale II-A	Scale III
		A	B	C			
Library Technical Assistant:							
FA 2 - Selection and Acquisition	4,5,6	3-4	-	3,4,5	2-4	3	2,3,4,7,8,10,12
FA 3 - Cataloging and Processing	4-6	2,3,4	-	3-5	2,3,4,5	3	2,3,4,7,10,12
FA 4 - Registration and Circulation	5	3-5	-	4	3,4	3	4,8,10
FA 5 - Reference Service	5	3-4	-	4-5	3	3	3,10
FA 6 - Patron Service	5	3-5	-	4	3-4	3	3,4,8,10
FA 7 - Collection Maintenance	4-6	3-4	-	3-5	2,3,4,5,6	2-3	2,3,4,9,10
Technical Assistant:							
Audio-Visual	4-6	2-4	2,3	3,4	2-6	2-3	2,3,4,9,10,12
Data Processing	5	2-4	2,3	4	1,4,6	2-3	3,12
Microfilming	3-5	3	2	2-5	2	2-3	2,3,10,12
Printing	4-5	2-4	2,3	3-4	2,3,4	2-3	2,3,4,7
Photography	3-4	2-3	2	3	2,3	3	2,3,9
Other	4,6	2-4	2,3	5	2-5	3	3,10
Library Associate	4-6	3-4	-	4-6	2-5	2,3	2,3,6,7,10,12
Associate Specialist	4-6	3-5	-	3-5	2-6	3	1,2,3,4,7,9,10,11,12
Associate Specialist or Specialist	4,5,6,7	3-4	3	4,5,6	4-6	3	2,4,5,7,10,11
Librarian:							
FA 1 - Administration	6,7	4,5	-	4,5	4,5,6,7	2-3	4,7,9,10
FA 2 - Selection and Acquisition	5,6,7,8	4,5	-	4-6	4,5,6,7	2-3	3,4,7,9,10
FA 3 - Cataloging and Processing	5-7	4-6	-	4-6	3-7	3	2,3,4,5,7,9,10
FA 4 - Registration and Circulation	5-6	4-5	-	4-5	4-7	3	4,9,10
FA 5 - Reference Services	5-7	4-5	-	4-5	3,4,5	3	2,6,7,9
FA 6 - Patron Services	5,6,7	4-5	-	4-6	4,5,6,7	3	4,5,6,7,9,10,11
FA 7 - Collection Maintenance	5,6,7	4-5	-	4-5	2,4,6,7	3	4,9,10

CHART B - continued

Position Categories	Scale VII	Scale V			Scale VI	Scale II-A	Scale III
		A	B	C			
Specialist:							
General Management	7,8	4,5	4,5,6	5-6	5,7,8	3	4,7,9,10, 12
Personnel	6-8	4,5,6	3-6	4,5,6	4-8(6)	2,3	2,4,7,9,10
Public Relations	5,6,7	4,5	2-3	4,5,6	4,6,7	2,3	4,7,9,12
Computer	5,6,7	4,5	6	4,5	1,4,5,6,7	3	2,4,10,12
Audio-Visual	6,7	3,4,5	2-6	4,5	6	2,3	2,4,7,10
Librarian or Specialist	6,7	4-5	2-5	4-6	4-8(6)	1,3	3,4,5,7, 9,10 & 11
Senior Librarian:							
FA 1 - Administration	6-8	4,5,6	-	5,6	4-8	3	4,5,7,8, 9,10
FA 2 - Selection and Acquisition	6-8	5	-	4-6	4,6,7,8	3	4,7,9,10
FA 3 - Cataloging and Processing	7-8	5,6	-	6	7	3	9,10
FA 6 - Patron Services	6,7	4,5	-	5,6	4,7	3	4
Senior Librarian or Senior Specialist:							
Professional	7,8	5,6	3,5,6	6	6,7	3	4,9,10
General Management	6,7,8	4,5,6	3-5	6	5-8	2,3	4,7,9,10 12
Buildings/Architecture	6,7,8	5-6	3,5	5,6	4-8	2,3	9,10
Budget/Fiscal	6,7,8	5,6	5	5,6	5,6,7,8	2,3	3,4,7,9, 10

Analysis of the SERD scales revealed the following:

Scale VII - Training Requirements: The characteristic range for Clerk positions was 1-4, with a few 5's, thus fitting easily the policy statement's requirement of high school graduation. The tasks described as Secretarial, Fiscal, and Personnel and Payroll had a somewhat higher 3-6 range, with Typing and Supplies positions and those in Functional Area 4 concerned with Overdues/Fines in a 3-5 range. Those called Supervisory Clerical ranged from 5 to 7.

Tasks placed in the Library Technical Assistant category fell in the 4-6 range, with most at the 5 level, and those grouped as Technical Assistants ranged from 3-6. While not going much beyond the level of high school graduation there was, at least, a visibly and consistently higher requirement here than for most of the Clerk positions.

Tasks grouped under both Library Associate and Associate Specialist also fell in the same 4-6 range, with only a few in the Associate Specialist or Specialist category going as high as 7. This would seem not quite to match the requirements established by the policy statement.

Librarian tasks had a 5-7 range, with a few stray 8's, rather than the clear-cut 7 one might have wished for, and the Specialists were the same, with a few more 8's. Again, however, there was a clear line of differentiation between these positions and the nonprofessional ones.

The Senior-level positions, Librarian or Specialist, were all in the 6-8 range, again consistent with each other and a cut above the journeyman-level tasks in their categories.

Scale V - General Educational Development: A similar gradual upward
progression was visible on Scale A (Reasoning), with the Clerks ranging 1-3, with
the exceptions again of Secretarial, Fiscal, and Personnel and Payroll, which
ranged 3-4, as did the Supervisory Clerical. The Library Technical Assistants
ranged generally 3-4, with an occasional 5, but the range for Technical Assistants
was only 2-4. The Associates (both Library and Specialist) also struck a 3-4 level,
with a few 5's. The Librarians hit a consistent 4-5, as did the Specialists with a
few stray 3's and 6's. The Senior levels ranged 4-6, with a predominance of 5's
and 6's.

Scale B (Mathematics) was tabulated for only a few categories, with
"high school mathematics" required only in the Fiscal grouping among the Clerks.
"Highly specialized mathematics" was required for no task listed. "Elementary
college mathematics" was required for a variety of Specialist tasks and in all
Senior-level groupings, but was dominant only in the Computer group.

Scale C (Language) again showed a gradual rise from 1-3 for the Unskilled
Clerical, to 3-4 for most tasks in the Clerk category. Level 5 ("Post high-school
and linguistic experience") began showing up in the Library Technical Assistant
tasks, but not as frequently in those of Technical Assistants. It was only at the
professional level (Librarian and Specialist) that 6's ("Considerable education
and linguistic experience") appeared with any frequency and they became more dominant at the Senior level.

Scale VI - Worker Instructions: Level 5 ("the worker is expected to know and employ theory...") did not occur until the Supervisory Clerical and Library Technical Assistant levels, and it occurred in only two of the six Functional Area groupings of LTA's. It occurred spottily among the Technical Assistants. Level 6 ("requires some creative use of theory well beyond referring to standard sources...") occurred occasionally among Supervisory Clerical, Library Technical Assistant, Technical Assistant, and Associate Specialist, but became dominant only at the Librarian level. It was here also that Level 7 (worker must define need or problem) appeared for the first time. Tasks at the Specialist level ranged widely, from 4-8, with 6 probably the most frequent level. All tasks at the Senior levels included some 7's and 8's, but again with a scattering of lower levels.

Scale II-A - Who or What Sets the Standards?:   With the exception of three tasks coded 1 ("the worker"), [2/] all were coded either 2 ("other") or 3 ("out-side criteria"). The 3's became dominant in Supervisory Clerical, Library Technical Assistant, Associate, Librarian, Specialist, and Senior categories.

Scale III - Task Environment: Most Clerk tasks were coded 2-3 ("repetitive, short cycle operations" performed "under specific instructions.") Those in the Administrative: Fiscal category, however, were significant exceptions, as were those in all the "over-the-desk" Registration and Circulation tasks. Beginning at the Supervisory Clerical/Library Technical Assistant levels, there was a wide mix, with 3 dropping out, with rare exceptions, at the professional levels.

2/ Two self-development items and one questionable one.

Conclusions and Recommendations

Without exception, the tasks included in the study were those traditionally performed in libraries, traditionally described. They fell easily into
the categories established in Library Education and Manpower. The line between
Clerk and Library Technical Assistant was clear and followed the definitions estab-
listed by the policy statement and the several Deininger Committee reports. 3/
Groupings of tasks emerged which logically could be described as Technical Assistants,
Associates, and Specialists. There was no difficulty in determining the base line
for tasks which were professional - either Librarian or Specialist.

The check against the five SERD scales revealed a structure roughly
resembling that described in the policy statement.

CHART C

	Clerk	L T A	T A	Assoc.	Lib.	Spec.	Sr. Lib./ Sr. Spec.
8							x x
7					x x	x x	x x
6		x	x x	x xx	x xx	x xx	xxxx
5		x xx	x xx	x xx	xxxx	xxxx	xxx
4	x xx	xxxx	xxxx	xxxx	xxx	xxx	x̄
3	xxxx	xxx	xxxx	xxx			
2	xxxx	x	x x	x			
1	xxxx		x				

The first column of x's in each category represents the predominant coding
for Scale VII; the second, Scale V-A; the third, V-C; and the fourth,
Scale VI. Scales II-A and III do not lend themselves to this type of
representation.

3/ See ALA Bulletin 62: 387-97, April, 1968; and "Criteria for Programs to
   Prepare Library/Media Technical Assistants," approved by the Board of
   Directors of the Library Education Division, American Library Association,
   June, 1971.

In any consideration of SERD's scales, it must be remembered that Scale X - Knowledge/Skills/Abilities Required is lacking. If present, this would undoubtedly create a sharper differentiation among the categories.

Before accepting this tentative fit, however, several other observations need to be made:

(1) A very high proportion of the tasks included in the study were clerical (46% including Supervisory Clerical).

(2) A significant number of the clerical tasks in the Administrative area, particularly in the Secretarial, Fiscal, and Personnel and Payroll subdivisions, were in the LTA rather than Clerical ranges on several of the SERD scales (most notably VII and V-A and C).

(3) A primary factor in raising either a Librarian or Specialist position to the Senior level was administrative responsibility, with size of unit or library a dominant factor.

(4) Although LTA/TA and Library Associate/Associate Specialist tasks were rated at similar levels on SERD's scales, the latter are by their nature tasks assignable to trainees or assistants, while the former grow out of similar work performed at lower levels.

(5) SERD's scales do not include the accountability or level of responsibility factor. Nor is there any weighting of factors to indicate relative importance.

A synthesis of all of these factors suggests that, on the basis of the tasks <u>described in this study</u>, the following career structure would be appropriate:

<u>Level 1</u>   <u>Clerk</u>

> Including all those tasks matching the general definition supplied by the policy statement and ranging generally in the 1-4 levels of SERD's scales VII, V-A and C, and VI.

<u>Level 2</u>   <u>Library</u>, <u>Technical</u>, and
                          <u>Administrative Assistants</u>

> Including all those tasks matching the general definition supplied by the policy statement and here sorted into LTA and TA categories, <u>plus</u> those separated experimentally as <u>Supervisory Clerical</u>, <u>plus</u> those in <u>Fiscal</u>, <u>Secretarial</u>, and <u>Personnel and Payroll</u> categories which range beyond the Clerk level in SERD's codings.

<u>Also at Level 2</u>   <u>Associates</u> - both Library and Specialist

> As defined in the policy statement and evaluated in this study.

<u>Level 3</u>   <u>Librarian/Specialist</u>

> As defined in the policy statement and evaluated in this study.

<u>Level 4</u>   <u>Senior Librarian/Senior Specialist</u>

> As defined in the policy statement and evaluated in this study.

The qualification requirements (apart from personal attributes) for these levels would be as follows:

Clerk:
High School graduation the basic requirement, plus requisite skills in typing, etc. as required by particular positions (may be acquired in high school, business school, on-the-job training or by other means).

Library, Technical and
  Administrative Assistants:
High school graduation plus the particular skills, knowledges, and judgment required by particular positions. These may be acquired through experience, in-service training or formal post-high school instruction in appropriate areas, and, most usually and most desirably, through a combination of these.

Associates:
B.A. or B.S. degree (with or without library science courses, as appropriate for particular positions).

Librarian:
M.L.S. degree.

Specialist:
Master's degree in field of specialization or bachelor's degree in appropriate field plus significant related experience (in or outside of libraries).

Senior Librarian:
M.L.S. degree, considerable breadth and depth of library experience, plus additional formal study, with (for the tasks described in this study) strong emphasis on management. A master's degree in management or other appropriate related field highly desirable.

There were no Senior Specialist tasks identified in this study. For those called "Senior Specialist or Senior Librarian," the requirements are essentially the same as for Senior Librarian - substantial experience on the base of a master's degree in the primary discipline, plus advanced formal study in a "cross" field.

The resulting structure of career progression would thus take the following approximate shape:

CHART D

Lines of Promotion

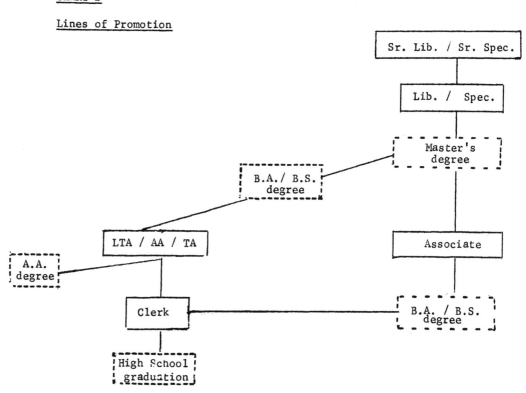

How, then, does this compare with the recommendations of the policy statement on Library Education and Manpower?

1.   There is complete agreement with the policy statement's definition of Clerk and its educational requirements. The pulling out of the upper ranges of some of the administrative tasks into an Administrative Assistant category is important, however. Because such tasks are smaller in number than those of similar levels of difficulty in the bibliographic area, they tend to be less visible and thus are viewed as "just clerical." Such duties as control of the library's accounts or its personnel record-keeping (including position and budgetary control, as well as the entire complex of salary increments, service ratings, etc.), along with the important interpersonal relationships involved, or serving as secretary to the director of the library, including supportive services to his relationship with the library board, require a very high level not only of skill, but of organization, responsibility, and above all, judgment. They fully merit recognition at a level equivalent to that of the Library Technical Assistant.

2.   There is complete agreement with the policy statement's definition of Library Technical Assistant, so far as the nature of the tasks performed is concerned, and strong support for the removal of such tasks from the Librarian level. Serious question is raised, however, regarding the educational requirements, especially as accompanied by the statement, "The Technical Assistant categories... are not meant simply to accommodate advanced clerks." While Clerks are not excluded by the policy statement from moving to the LTA level (indeed, the career-lattice diagram indicates this as a line of promotion for them), the basic requirements established for the level recognize only formal study, not the learnings which come through experience.

What is being recommended here is that primary recognition be given to valid related experiential learning, with the two-year college program still recognized as an alternative but not necessarily a more desirable mode of entry. The advanced

clerk should indeed be strongly encouraged (or in some cases required) to undertake

formal course work to assist in his development to the LTA level. Courses directly

concerned with library techniques might well provide a valuable synthesis and over-

view of that which he has learned on the job. Or, even more profitably, he might

take courses in supervision, or in computer applications to library processes, or

some other subject which has <u>not</u> been taught in the course of his clerical assign-

ments.

There are two reasons for this emphasis on stronger recognition of experi-

ence as a qualification for promotion to the Library Technical Assistant level.

One is the nature of the LTA tasks themselves, and the other is the high proportion

of library tasks which are clerical.

The LTA tasks represent the highest level on a continuum and are different

from the tasks immediately below them in the Clerk category only in degree of complex-

ity. Those tasks requiring the kinds of knowledge provided by general education are

already excluded from this category. It would therefore seem that an able clerk,

after a number of years of well planned, well evaluated, well supervised experience

would be the natural candidate for advancement to the LTA level, and would bring to

his performance a more substantially based judgment.

In analyzing any career structure, the amount of work to be performed, or

the number of staff employed to do it, at any level, is also of significance.

For example, the career line of a photographer in a typical library is extremely

short; there just is not that much photography to be performed. There need to be

more ladders up from a category containing two hundred positions than from one in-

cluding twenty. This kind of quantitative information was not provided in the Phase I

document, and it is not altogether safe to use the total number of tasks in any one

category as a criterion. Some of the tasks described are very simple and specific,
requiring only a few minutes to perform, while others are complex and general,
almost unmeasurable in terms of time requirements. Nevertheless, the ratio
represented by such a mechanical count can provide insights.

	No. of Tasks	% of Total	CHART E
Sr. Lib. or Sr. Spec.	50	(6.0%)	
Senior Librarian	41	(4.9%)	
Librarian or Specialist	24	(2.8%)	
Specialist	67	(8.0%)	
Librarian	119	(14.5%)	
Assoc.Spec. or Specialist	15	(1.8%)	
Associate Specialist	15	(1.8%)	
Library Associate	14	(1.7%)	
TA,LTA,Superv. Clerical	135	(16.0%)	
Non-Supervisory Clerical	360	(43.0%)	

Numerically, the clerks are the backbone of the library staff, and to cut
off their primary promotional line by the insertion of another category, itself
sharply limited in upward potential, does a serious disservice to both. There is a
good numerical ratio between the two levels, however, if one is regarded as the
natural base for the other.

While the policy statement does not actually rule out the kind of advancement proposed here, neither does it expressly permit it, and it is apparent in the
field that instead of relieving the denigration of clerical work long prevalent in
libraries, the recognition of the LTA category has added another layer of staff to
join in it.

3. There is no disagreement with the definition or educational requirements established by the policy statement for Library Associate/Associate Specialist, but there is disagreement with its placement as a category. The SERD scales place it on an exact par with the Technical Assistant level, and this is where it belongs. It is, at least so far as the tasks included in this study are concerned, purely and simply a trainee level. While the duties require the general education represented by the bachelor's degree, they do not require experience nor are they at the level of responsibility represented by the LTA/TA/AA tasks.

4. The Librarian category produced no problems or disagreement.

5. The Specialist category is one which has long needed the formal recognition in libraries which the policy statement now provides. The master's degree established as the basic requirement by the policy statement is highly desirable and should be strongly encouraged. It is for the most part completely justified by the tasks described here. The only reason for proposing the possible alternative of bachelor's degree in the field of specialization plus significant related experience is that all of the fields represented do not parallel precisely the educational patterns established for librarianship, and there are many conceivable situations, particularly in libraries of the size and type represented here, in which otherwise highly qualified persons would not meet the formal requirement of a master's degree. What is probably most important in these positions, along with basic professional competence, is the capacity to understand and relate to the concerns of libraries, and this, in a sense creates a dual demand to start with. The requirement of significant related experience beyond the bachelor's degree balances the MLS without experience required of the Librarian.

6. There was complete agreement with the policy statement at the Senior Librarian/Senior Specialist level. The tasks placed in the Senior Librarian category were largely at the policy level and almost entirely administrative in nature. Those described as Senior Librarian or Senior Specialist represented high levels of responsibility which could be assumed by librarians or specialists, depending on such variables as: (1) whether the library had a business manager, for example, or the library director handled the budget-making process directly; (2) interpretation of the task (for example, "checks and evaluates library programs in relation to professional standards," which could be done by a librarian for the library's programs of public service or by a personnel specialist for the library's personnel programs); (3) functions for which responsibility could rest with either librarian or specialist, but which by their very nature involve close coordination (as between public relations specialist and librarian in "monitors and supervises staff presentations related to library programs on radio station."). The flexibility of educational requirements provided by the policy statement at this level was particularly appropriate, since practically all of the tasks included here would call for advanced study in other areas rather than an additional degree in library science.

7. Movement among categories is perhaps not indicated with complete clarity by either this study or the policy statement. The inclusion here of the category Associate Specialist or Specialist provides an example in which the tasks would be performed by the Specialist if he had no assistant, but which could well be delegated to one just entering or seeking to enter the field of specialization. Similarly, although not formally indicated, the line between Librarian/Senior Librarian or Specialist/Senior Specialist would be drawn in different places depending on the size of the library or unit, or the stage of development of the incumbent of the position. These shadings can be seen more clearly in actual practice, involving

total positions, not isolated tasks, and actual incumbents, not theoretical
"categories of manpower." This is the essence of intelligent manpower utilization.
Suffice it to say here that no task should be considered immutably, at all times
and places, to be in one category or another, at one level or another. To inter-
pret either this or similar studies, or the policy statement itself, thus literally
and inflexibly would be the surest way to cut off growth and development of staff.[4]

There are, in fact, two distinct career services, separated by a very firm
line which can be crossed only through the attainment of the level of general education represented by the bachelor's degree. On the one side are the positions beginning with Clerk and rising to the top levels of the LTA/TA categories. With a number
of grades within each category, this constitutes a viable career structure for
high school graduates, who should be expected to improve their skills and broaden
their educational backgrounds as they move to positions of greater responsibility.
On the other side is the professional structure, beginning with Associate or trainee
positions, reaching the professional level with the attainment, in most cases, of
the master's degree, and continuing to rise on the basis of increasingly higher
levels of responsibility, accompanied by continuing education appropriate to the
position requirements.

This essentially is both the pattern established in the policy statement
and the one recommended by this study.

---

[4] This is undoubtedly what is intended by the various arrows on the career lattice
diagram (Figure 2) of the policy statement. Yet somehow these arrows create confusion, because they imply a freedom of upward movement not actually possible except as
educational requirements are met at each stage of advancement. Similarly, the horizontal arrows indicating lateral movement - between Library Technical Assistant and
Technical Assistant, Librarian and Specialist, Senior Librarian and Senior Specialist-
seem to be in conflict with the concept of specialization built up through the series
of educational requirements.

The principal line of disagreement is between the policy statement's emphasis on academic achievement as the "single best means for determining that an applicant has the background recommended for each category" and the point of view of this study that experience - - guided, planned, and evaluated experience - - is, for several of the categories, a factor of at least equal importance.

The strict adherence to formal educational standards is easier for an administrator, but in the flux of daily practice and staffing needs, and particularly in the light of the diverse array of talents represented on any staff, other factors will always need to be considered.

The policy statement is concerned with categories of manpower, and the approach of this study is through tasks performed. It is, in the final analysis, the work performed which is at one level or another, and the ultimate test of the individual's qualifications is not the precise amount of pre- or in-service training or experience per se, but the totality of both as expressed through performance.

*   *   *

Once again, it must be emphasized that this study is based on the tasks performed in a specific group of small- to medium-sized public libraries, as described in the Phase I document of the Task Analysis Project. No metropolitan public libraries, school, special, college or university libraries were included. While the methodology may be applied to tasks in any library, the model and recommendations will not have universal application.

GLOSSARY

Accountability   Establishing goals, setting specific objectives, devising programs to meet the objectives, carrying out the programs, measuring their degree of success, comparing costs and performance under alternate programs, revising and trying again. . . . Proof from the . . . system that it is doing what it is supposed to do.

WOODINGTON, p. 95.

. . . a negotiated relationship in which the participants agree in advance to accept specified awards and costs on the basis of evaluation findings as to the attainment of specified ends.

ALKIN, p. 2.

Career Lattice   . . . utilizes the interrelationships among jobs to create promotional opportunities and facilitate mobility of workers among jobs. A career lattice provides for mobility in three directions: horizontal mobility to jobs at the same relative level of complexity but in a different area of work, vertical mobility to more complex jobs in the same area of work, and diagonal mobility to more complex jobs in a different but related area of work.

U.S. Dept. of Labor, *A Handbook for Job Restructuring,* p. 2.

Differentiated Staffing   . . . implies dividing the global role of the [librarian] into professional and paraprofessional subroles according to specific functions and duties to be performed . . . and according to particular talents and strengths evident within the human resources of any given [library] community.

COOPER, p. 1.

Element   The smallest step into which it is practicable to subdivide any work activity without analyzing separate motions, movements, and mental processes involved.

U.S. Dept. of Labor, *Handbook for Analyzing Jobs,* p. 3.

Evaluation   Evaluation is the process of determining the kinds of decisions that have to be made and selecting, collecting, and interpreting the information needed in making these decisions.

KLEIN, A-2.

The process of delineating, obtaining, and providing useful information for judging decision alternatives.

Stufflebeam, "Relevance of the CIPP Evaluation Model," p. 19.

Factor Ranking . . . essentially a technique of comparing the job to be evaluated with all others, one factor at a time.
U.S. Civil Service Commission,
Report of the Job Evaluation and Pay Review Task Force, p. 355-56.

Goal The general target or aim from which several objectives are derived.
ROUECHE, p. 24.

Job . . . a group of positions which are identical with respect to their major or significant tasks and sufficiently alike to justify their being covered by a single analysis. There may be one or many persons employed in the same job.
U.S. Dept. of Labor, *Handbook for Analyzing Jobs,* p. 3.

Job Analysis . . . the systematic process of collecting and making certain judgments about all of the pertinent information relating to the nature of a specific job.
U.S. Civil Service Commission, *Job Analysis,* p. 3.

Job Design See *Job Restructuring.*

Job Restructuring . . . a special application of job analysis that involves the identification of jobs within the context of the system of which they are a part and the analysis and rearrangement of their tasks to achieve a desired purpose.
U.S. Dept. of Labor, *A Handbook for Job Restructuring,* p. 1.

Job Rotation . . . planned movement . . . from one position to another for the purpose of encouraging . . . development and growth.
MORRIS, p. 1.

Methods Verbs . . . used to denote the specific methods of performing the work.
U.S. Dept. of Labor, *Handbook for Analyzing Jobs,* p. 4-5.

Objectives An aim or end of action.
Granger, p. 63.

Position . . . a collection of tasks constituting the total work assignment of a single worker. There are as many positions as there are workers.
U.S. Dept. of Labor, *Handbook for Analyzing Jobs,* p. 3.

Position Analysis See *Job Analysis; Position.*

Position Classification . . . [the] grouping together in categories or classes of those positions which are sufficiently similar in duties and responsibilities so that they can be treated alike for administrative purposes.
U.S. Civil Service Commission, *Job Analysis,* p. 7.

Program A sequence of action steps arranged in the priority necessary to accomplish an objective.
ROUECHE, p. 24.

Purpose The basic reason for an organization's existence.
ROUECHE, p. 24.

Subsystem See *Program.*

Systems Analysis	. . . a formal procedure for examining a complex process or organization, reducing it to its component parts, and relating these parts to each other and to the unit as a whole in accordance with an agreed-upon performance criterion. Borko, p. 37.
Task	. . . one or more elements and . . . one of the distinct activities that constitute logical and necessary steps in the performance of work by the worker. A task is created whenever human effort, physical or mental, is exerted to accomplish a specific purpose. U.S. Dept. of Labor, *Handbook for Analyzing Jobs,* p. 3.
Task Analysis	See *Job Analysis; Task.*

BIBLIOGRAPHY

The following references are supplementary to those provided in the footnotes throughout the text.

"Accountability." *Journal of Research and Development in Education,* Fall 1971 (entire issue). 100 p.

Alkin, Marvin C. "Accountability Defined." Published by U.C.L.A. Center for the Study of Evaluation in *Evaluation Comment,* May 1972, p. 1-5.

American Library Association. American Association of School Librarians. School Library Manpower Project. *Behavioral Requirements Analysis Checklist: A Compilation of Competency Based Job Functions and Task Statements for School Library Media Personnel.* Chicago: The Association, 1973. 72 p.

————. *Occupational Definitions for School Library Media Personnel.* Chicago: The Association, 1971. 24 p.

————. *School Library Personnel: Task Analysis Survey.* Chicago: The Association, 1969. 91 p.

Bartlett, Alton C., and Kayser, Thomas A., eds. *Changing Organizational Behavior.* Englewood Cliffs, N.J.: Prentice-Hall, 1973. 434 p.

Barrett, Jon H. *Individual Goals and Organizational Objectives: A Study of Integration Mechanisms.* Ann Arbor: Univ. of Michigan Institute for Social Research, 1970. 151 p.

Benge, Ronald C. *Libraries and Cultural Change.* Hamden, Conn.: Archon Books, 1970, p. 222-43 (chapter 13).

Bone, Larry Earl. "Study in Renewal: A Library in Search of Itself." *Library Journal,* March 1, 1972, p. 844-47.

Borko, Harold. "Design of Information Systems and Services." *Annual Review of Information Science and Technology,* 1967.

Burness, Carl G. *Defining Library Objectives.* Detroit: Wayne State Univ., 1968 (ERIC no. ED 045 116).

Civil Service Assembly of the United States and Canada. Committee on Position-Classification and Pay Plans in the Public Service. *Position-Classification in the Public Service.* 6th printing. Chicago: Public Personnel Assn., 1965. 404 p.

Cooper, James Michael. *Differentiated Staffing.* Philadelphia: Saunders, 1972. 147 p.

Dallas Public Library. *Library Service Goals 1972-1982.* Dallas: The Library, 1972. 8 p.

Davis, Keith. *Human Behavior at Work: Human Relations and Organizational Behavior.* 4th ed. New York: McGraw-Hill, 1972. 584 p.

Davis, Louis E., and Taylor, James C., eds. *Design of Jobs: Selected Readings.* Baltimore: Penguin Books, 1972. 479 p.

English, Fenwick W., and Sharpes, Donald K. *Strategies for Differentiated Staffing.* Berkeley: McCutchan, 1972. 381 p.

Francis, G. James. "The Reciprocity of Organizational Climate." *Advanced Management Journal,* October 1973, p. 46-51.

Granger, Charles H. "The Hierarchy of Objectives." *Harvard Business Review,* May-June 1964, p. 63-74.

11696
5-10

Gross, Bertram M., ed. *Social Intelligence for America's Future: Explorations in Societal Problems.* Boston: Allyn and Bacon, 1969. 541 p.

Hage, Jerald, and Aiken, Michael. "Routine Technology, Social Structure, and Organization Goals." *Administrative Science Quarterly,* September 1969, p. 366-76.

Hamburg, Morris, et al. "Library Objectives and Performance Measures and Their Use in Decision Making." *Library Quarterly,* January 1972, p. 107-28.

Herzberg, Frederick. *Work and the Nature of Man.* Cleveland, O.: World Publishing, 1966. 203 p.

Hostrop, Richard W. *Managing Education for Results.* Homewood, Ill.: ETC Publications, 1973. 248 p.

Howell, Robert A. "Managing by Objectives—A Three-Stage System." *Business Horizons,* February 1970, p. 41-45.

Huizinga, Gerard. *Maslow's Need Hierarchy in the Work Situation.* Groningen, The Netherlands: Wolters-Noordhoff, 1970. 207 p.

Kahn, A.M.C. "Objectives." *Library Association Record,* May 1970, p. 191-93.

Klein, Stephen B. *Evaluation Workshop I: Participants' Notebook.* Monterey, Cal.: CTB/McGraw-Hill, 1971.

Koontz, Harold, and O'Donnell, Cyril. *Management: A Book of Readings.* 3d ed. New York: McGraw-Hill, 1972. 816 p.

Lawless, David J. *Effective Management: Social Psychological Approach.* Englewood Cliffs, N.J.: Prentice-Hall, 1972. 422 p.

Liesener, James W. "The Development of a Planning Process for Media Programs." *School Media Quarterly,* Summer 1973, p. 278-87.

Mahrer, John R., ed. *New Perspectives in Job Enrichment.* New York: Van Nostrand, Reinhold, 1971. 226 p.

Martin, Lowell A. *Library Response to Urban Change.* Chicago: American Library Assn., 1969, p. 14-23 (chapter 2).

Massachusetts Department of Education. Bureau of Library Extension. "Guide to the Employment of Professional and Sub-Professional Personnel in Massachusetts Public Libraries." Mimeographed. Boston: The Department, 1972. 10 p.

McConkey, Dale D. "Applying Management by Objectives to Non-Profit Organizations." *Advanced Management Journal,* January 1973, p. 10-20.

Morris, James. *Job Rotation: A Study and Program.* Occasional Papers in Management, Organization, Industrial Relations, no. 11. Chicago: Univ. of Chicago Industrial Relations Center, 1957. 16 p.

National Education Association. Association for Educational Communications and Technology. *Jobs in Instructional Media.* 2d printing. Washington, D.C.: The Association, 1971. 304 p.

Penzer, William N. "After Everyone's Had His Job Enriched, Then What?" *Administrative Management,* October 1973, p. 20-22, 76, 78.

———. *Productivity and Motivation Through Job Engineering.* American Management Association management briefing. New York: AMACOM, 1973. 31 p.

Raths, Louis E., et al. *Values and Teaching.* Columbus, O.: Charles E. Merrill, 1966. 275 p.

Roueche, John E.; Baker, George A. III; and Brownell, Richard L. *Accountability and the Community College.* Washington, D.C.: American Association of Junior Colleges, 1971.

Simon, Herbert A. "On the Concept of Organizational Goals." *Administrative Science Quarterly,* June 1964, p. 1-22.

Simon, Sidney B. *Values Clarification.* New York: Hart, 1972. 397 p.

Stufflebeam, Daniel L. "Relevance of the CIPP Evaluation Model for Educational Accountability." *Journal of Research and Development in Education,* Fall 1971, p. 19-25.

Tosi, Henry L.; Rizzo, John R.; and Carroll, Stephen J. "Setting Goals in Management by Objectives." *California Management Review,* Summer 1970, p. 70-78.

Tulsa City-County Library. "Long Range Plans: A Ten-Year Projection." 8th draft. Mimeographed. Tulsa: The Library, 1973. 23 p.

U.S. Civil Service Commission. Bureau of Intergovernmental Personnel Programs. *Job Analysis: Key to Better Management.* Washington, D.C.: Govt. Print. Off., 1973. 12 p.

U.S. Department of Health, Education, and Welfare. Office of Education. National Center for Educational Communication. *Educational Accountability and Evaluation.* PREP Report no. 35. Washington, D.C.: Govt. Print. Off., 1972.

Wasserman, Paul, and Bundy, Mary Lee, eds. *Reader in Library Administration.* Washington, D.C.: Microcard Editions, 1968, p. 123-78 (part III).

Wiley, Wretha W., and Fine, Sidney A. *An Introduction to Functional Job Analysis: A Scaling of Selected Tasks from the Social Welfare Field.* Kalamazoo, Mich.: W. E. Upjohn Institute for Employment Research, 1971. 87 p.

Woodington, Donald D. "Accountability from the Viewpoint of a State Commissioner of Education." *Phi Delta Kappan,* October 1972, p. 95-97.

Wren, Daniel A. *The Evolution of Management Thought.* New York: Ronald Press, 1972. 556 p.